THE HA

BOOK OF

C000218888

ABRAHAM HOCHWALD
Translated by Anne Moellers

HarperCollins*Publishers*

HarperCollins*Publishers*
77–85 Fulham Palace Road, London W6 8JB

First published in Germany in 1994 by
R. Brockhaus, Verlag GmbH and Co. KG.
This edition published in Great Britain in 1996 by
HarperCollins*Publishers*

3 5 7 9 10 8 6 4 2

A catalogue record for this book is
available from the British Library

0 00 627999 6

Printed and bound in Great Britain by
Caledonian International Book Manufacturing Ltd, Glasgow

CONTENTS

✡

About the Author   v
Introduction   VII

The Talmud   1
The Middle Ages   3
Anti-Semitism   10
The Assimilation   19
Rabbis   24
Match-making and married life   35
Money matters   45
The *nouveaux riches*   60
Doctors and patients   64
Jews in the army   69
Nazi Germany   75
The Soviet Union   84
The United States   101
Israel   116
Miscellaneous   143

ABOUT THE AUTHOR

✡

Abraham Hochwald was born in 1923 in Trieste, Italy (then part of the Austro-Hungarian Empire). He studied the Talmud at Montreux in Switzerland and at Jerusalem, and read Sociology and English Literature at the Hebrew University in Jerusalem. After working for the Israeli Ministry for Social Affairs, he became Director for the Department of Religious Education at the Agence Juive in southern France. Later he worked as a rabbi in various parts of Germany. He has mastered eight languages, holds a diploma in translation and has written a number of commentaries on the Bible and articles on the essence of Judaism. Through several publications in Germany he has made a name for himself as an expert in Jewish humour.

INTRODUCTION

✡

People generally like to mock the weaknesses of their contemporaries: they ridicule the mean Scots, the monosyllabic English, the talkative Italians, the pompous newly rich, the sad stutterer, the pedantic bureaucrat and so on. In contrast to that, Jews mainly laugh at themselves, at the fate which has subjected them for two millennia to the rule of foreigners who have persistently embittered their lives. They have laughed at the poverty which so often was their fate, caused by constant wandering and by the limitations imposed on their trade or work. They have mocked those among their co-religionists who had no command of Hebrew at all and who made bad mistakes when reading the Bible or the prayer-book. Jews have even invented their own 'Irish' in the form of a little city in Poland: in 'Chelm' all inhabitants – from the mayor to the water-carrier – were fools at whose expense one could laugh. The fact that a city needed to be invented to provide fools for the Jews to laugh at shows how rare they were in real life!

The hallmarks of the Jewish joke are its sharp and often unexpected point, and the tragi-comic situation which is its theme, intentionally overdone to the point of absurdity. It often has a bitter smack because it is built on self-pity. However, the Jewish joke always has a therapeutic effect: it ridicules suffering and tension, thereby making them easier to bear. It turns the tormentor into a figure of ridicule and it mocks hunger and misery, thus removing their sting.

The Jew has the gift of immediately adjusting himself to any new situation and humorously commenting on it. For example, in the first years of the Nazi regime a flood of Jewish anti-Nazi jokes appeared, ridiculing the new rulers and their racial laws. This was the only possible form of resistance against the brutal dictatorship. Similarly in Russia, when they came to power the Communists used brutal force to prevent the Jews from pursuing their religion and culture. Thus, on the one side the Jewish anti-brown joke and on the other side the Jewish anti-red joke were created – both attacking the totalitarian regimes with biting irony, though only verbally and behind closed doors.

The establishment of the modern Jewish state after nineteen centuries of diaspora opened up new horizons to Jewish humour and gave to it a wealth of new impulses. There now appeared the specifically Israeli joke – a masterly type of comment on this completely new political situation. Israeli humour found its victims among the new immigrants and their difficulties with integration, among the members of the new but already advanced governmental bureaucracy, as well as among brash American tourists. Each phase in the development of the state of Israel found its matching expression in an Israeli joke. Thus the food rationing ordered by the government in the years 1949–52 was bitterly commented upon. It became necessary because of the mass immigration of North African Jews and the resulting food shortage. On the other hand, the incredibly fast and overwhelming victory of the Israeli army against the forces of the boastful Egyptian President Gamal Abdul Nasser during the Six Day War in 1967 created a flood of ironic jokes which were even published in book form. In the 1980s, Israeli humour concentrated on the country's galloping 220% inflation, which was a world record – a success for which Israel had been vainly looking in the field of sporting endeavour...

At the same time a specifically American Jewish humour had developed in the United States. This humour mocked the language difficulties which the mostly Eastern European Yiddish-speaking immigrants faced. It also laughed at these immigrants' efforts to gain acceptance in established American society.

Jewish humour tends to be sharp, acerbic and witty, and Israel and America are today the places where it can be found in the greatest abundance.

I
THE TALMUD

Rabbi Seroka often went to the market-place in the city of Be-Lapat (in Chusistan), where the prophet Elijah used to appear to him. During one of these meetings two men passed by, and the prophet said to the rabbi: 'These two will get into heaven one day.'

A short time later the rabbi approached the two and asked them: 'What is your profession?'

They answered: 'We're comedians. When we meet someone who is depressed we cheer him up.'

✡

A Gentile philosopher once said to Rabbi Gamliel, 'Your God is a thief, because the Bible says that God put Adam into a deep sleep and then stole one of his ribs, and from it created Eve.'

At that, the daughter of Gamliel said to her father, 'Allow me to answer him!' Her father agreed, and she said to the philosopher, 'Someone please bring me a judge, because I have to report a theft! Last night a thief entered our house, stole a silver cup and left a gold one in its place.'

'I would like to be robbed by such thieves all the time!' exclaimed the philosopher.

'This,' answered the daughter, 'is exactly what happened to Adam, because although God took a rib from him, He gave him instead a lifelong companion who would stand by his side!'

A man from Athens was visiting Jerusalem. He gave some money to a child and told him to go and buy some eggs and some cheese. The boy raced away and soon returned with his purchases.

'Now, show me,' said the Athenian, who had heard about the cleverness of the people of Jerusalem, 'which cheese is from a white goat, and which is from a black goat.'

'I'll do that as soon as you show me which egg comes from a white hen, and which comes from a black hen!'

2

THE MIDDLE AGES

A special type of Jewish humour was formed in the relationship between the East-European village Jew and the Christian nobleman (the so-called 'Poretz') who owned the whole village. The Poretz ruled the lives of the Jews by the granting and removing of tenancies.

A Poretz would often keep a Jew as his factotum, whom he always called 'Moshka', no matter what his real name was, and on whom he liked to play foolish tricks. Here follows a classic example of such capricious behaviour, which also shows how a Jew could use it to his own benefit:

✡

The Poretz said to his protected Jew: 'Moshka, I want you to get me a fox terrier as soon as possible!'

'No problem,' said Moshka. 'I'll get you a fox terrier, but you know you can't get one for less than 400 roubles!'

'All right,' said the Poretz, 'here's the money.' Moshka hurried home, very pleased with himself.

When his wife asked what the Poretz wanted he said, 'Don't ask questions – today I made the deal of my life! All I have to do now is to find out what a fox terrier is!'

✡

*Another rich vein of Jewish humour has been the often
tense relationship between Jews and Christians. It
seems that again and again the medieval rulers were
tempted to force the Jews into debates with
representatives of the church.*

*In cases where the Jews lost a dispute, they were
threatened with expulsion from the city in question. So
it is easy to understand why Jewish scholars were very
reluctant to represent the Jewish side during such
disputes, a situation which is illustrated by the
following anecdote:*

The day of the annual disputation was drawing near,
and none of the Jewish scholars were willing to
represent their community. But Jankel the water carrier
said, 'If no one else will do it then I will.' The community
was horrified – should such an ignoramus be allowed
into such a discussion with a bishop? It would be a
disaster!

Finally, as no scholar had volunteered, the community
decided that it must send Jankel. They dressed him up as
a rabbi and hoped for a miracle.

The Bishop announced that the disputation was going
to be held in silence and would be conducted only by
gestures. It consisted of three points: if the Jew found the
three matching gestures, he would win.

The Bishop began the disputation by raising one
finger; immediately Jankel raised two fingers. The
Bishop then showed his open hand, at which Jankel
showed his fist. Finally, the Bishop raised a glass of red
wine, upon which Jankel took a piece of white cheese
out of his bag. Now, totally contrite, the Bishop

explained that the Jew had refuted all three points and had thereby won the disputation. There was great consternation among the Christians, but the Bishop praised the Jew as a great theologian and explained the contents of their theological disputation. First, he had raised one finger to show that the Christians as well as the Jews believed in one God. At that, the Jew had raised two fingers to say that the Christians believed in Father and Son and that therefore Christianity was not a truly monotheistic religion. Then the Bishop had shown his widely open fingers to indicate that the Jews had been scattered by God all over the world. Like the five fingers of his hand, they had been spread in all directions, and this would be the case for ever. But then the Jew had raised his fist to indicate that God would bring them all together one day and make them one people again.

Finally, the Bishop had shown red wine. Red is the colour of sin, and he had thereby called the Jews sinners whose sins God would never forgive. At that the Jew had taken the white cheese, indicating, as is said in the Scriptures, that 'Even if your sins are of deepest purple I will make them as white as wool.'

There was great celebration amongst the Jews and all were keen to know how the ignorant Jankel had managed to defeat the learned bishop. Jankel proudly explained the whole procedure from his point of view: 'Initially the Bishop provoked me by raising his finger as if to indicate that he would poke out my eye, so I raised two fingers to threaten him with poking out both of his. Then he raised his hand as if to threaten to hit me, so I raised my fist to make it clear that I would hit back. When he realized that I wasn't afraid of him he wanted to be reconciled with me and offered me a glass of red wine. So I took out a piece of white cheese because red wine and white cheese go well together!'

✡

The Count called for his Moshka. He said, 'Moshka, my dog is highly intelligent, and I want you to teach him Polish!'

'But Sir, how can I teach a dog Polish?' replied Moshka. 'It isn't a human being!'

'My dog is more clever than some people I know,' answered the Count. 'Moshka, this is an order, and if you refuse to obey me you can pack your things and leave right now!'

'All right, I'll do it, but I need time. Something like this isn't done overnight.'

'I'll give you one year!'

'Impossible! In one year I can't teach any dog a language. I demand five years!'

'Very well, then, in five years' time the dog must be able to lead a conversation in Polish!'

The Jew returned home and told his wife about the trouble he had been led into. His wife, worried, said, 'Are you crazy? How can you promise to teach a dog Polish?!'

'That's why I asked for five years,' he replied. 'In five years all sorts of things can happen. Either the dog or the Count will be dead!'

✡

A baptized Jew was brought before the Spanish Inquisition after it had discovered that he had secretly celebrated Passover.

'We will leave your fate in the hands of Divine Providence,' said the Grand Inquisitor. 'Here are two pieces of paper. On one is written "Death" and on the other "Life". You have to choose one of these two pieces!'

The Jew was convinced that "Death" was written on both pieces and that the whole procedure was nothing but a macabre farce. What could he do? Suddenly he was struck by a brilliant idea! He took one of the two pieces of paper and swallowed it. He said to his tormenter: 'I don't know what's written on the piece I swallowed, but it shouldn't be too difficult to find out. If the other one shows "Death", then I've drawn "Life"!'

Israel Zangwill tells an anecdote about two Spanish Jews at the time of the Inquisition. To save their lives they both decided to undergo baptism. They walked to the cathedral and asked for an audience with the bishop. As he was not immediately available, they decided to wait. One hour went by, then another, and soon it was sunset. At this, one of them said, 'If it takes much longer we'll miss the *Mincha*!'[1]

---

[1] The *Mincha* is the late-afternoon service which every devout Jew should attend daily.

3
ANTI-SEMITISM

In the Russian district of Horodno, during the time of Rabbi Nachum, there was a governor who didn't bother to hide his hatred of Jews and who persecuted the Jewish population. However, Rabbi Nachum was an exception: the governor respected him as a man of great scholarship and true piety.

At the annual New Year reception to which Rabbi Nachum was invited it was his habit to wish the governor success in the New Year. On one of these occasions, the governor asked the rabbi for a confidential talk. When they were finally alone, the governor said immediately, 'Don't think that I don't know that you hate me and that your good wishes are not meant. What surprises me is that you, whom I consider an honest and straight person, wish something for me which in your inner heart you don't mean.'

'You're wrong there,' replied Rabbi Nachum. 'The good wishes that we expressed came from the bottom of our hearts. What did we wish you? A year of success – and what does success mean for a man in your position? That you will climb even higher and will be promoted into the ministry. Then, you will have to move to St Petersburg and leave our city, and that is what we wish with all our hearts!'

During the reign of Czar Alexander III his anti-Semitic Minister Ignatjew enacted several anti-Jewish laws. At that time a rumour began to circulate to the effect that Baron Ginzburg, an ennobled Jew, had started collecting money to bribe Minister Ignatjew to make him repeal these laws.

When the two met, Ignatjew said to the Baron, 'I have heard that you want to offer me money, Baron. How much did you have in mind?'

Upon which the Baron said, 'Well, it can't be the value I place upon the Jews, as I don't have such a huge sum, but the value that you place upon them I can offer at any time!'

✡

The Polish King Stanislaus August appointed the Jew Issachar Halevy Lehmann as his Finance Minister. Some of his courtiers criticized this decision and openly expressed their surprise that the King should trust a Jew with power over the country's finances – after all, everyone knew that the Jews were greedy, as they had shown when they danced around the Golden Calf during the time of Moses. The King, who knew the biblical stories well, replied, 'You obviously don't know that the Jew Lehmann belongs to the tribe of Levy, of which the Bible says that it alone didn't take part in the worship of the Golden Calf!'

✡

Sir Moses Montefiore, a famous English Jewish philanthropist, was sitting next to an anti-Semitic aristocrat at a banquet. 'I have just returned from a trip to Japan,' said the anti-Semite, 'and to my surprise I discovered that they have neither Jews nor pigs in Japan.'

'Is that so?' responded Montefiore. 'In that case the two of us should settle in Japan so that they have at least one member of each species!'

✡

On another occasion Sir Moses Montefiore was visiting an anti-Semitic earl who showed his guests tricks performed by his highly trained dog. The Earl decided to pay back Montefiore for his lack of interest and called his dog, with a loud voice, 'Come here, Moshka!'

Montefiore turned to the earl and said, 'It's a pity that you've given the dog a Jewish name – otherwise he would have a good chance of advancement and perhaps might become an earl!'

✡

The Duke of Mannheim said to the Jewish scholar, Rabbi Isaac Brill, 'They say that Jews who come before the courts try to buy the favour of the judges with large amounts of money. Isn't it unjust to bribe the judge in order to bend the law?'

To which the Rabbi answered, 'The law isn't bent this way – on the contrary. Let me explain. When a Jew and a Christian have an argument and come to stand before a

Christian judge, it is natural that the judge, to start with, is prejudiced in favour of the Christian. The money that the Jewish party gives to him motivates the judge to steer his opinion away from the Christian and to become completely impartial!'

✡

When Professor Albert Einstein published his sensational Theory of Relativity, everyone spoke of the genius who had shaken the entire world of science. At the time Einstein said, 'Should my theory be proved valid, then Germany and France will fight over me. Germany will say that I'm a German and France will say that I'm a world citizen. Should the theory not prove true, Germany and France will still fight over me. France will say that I'm a German and Germany will say that I'm a Jew!'

✡

An elderly Jewish man who served his community as a religious teacher and butcher stood before a German judge who was known for his anti-Semitic views. During all the proceedings he never called the defendant by his name but referred to him only as 'Mr Butcher'. When the hearing was over, the judge asked the old man, 'Mr Butcher, do you wish to add anything to your statement?'

'Yes, Sir,' replied the man. 'I would like to emphasize that to humans I'm a teacher and only to beasts am I a butcher!'

Duzring the Peace Conference which took place after the First World War to redraw the borders within Europe, Louis Marshall (1856–1929), the leader of the American Jews, and Ignatz Paderewski, the leader of the Poles, were having a conversation. Paderewski said, 'Marshall, you have to use your influence on the Conference to safeguard Poland's interests. Otherwise, the Polish people will vent their anger on the Jews and will start having bloody pogroms.'

Marshall replied, 'If the Peace Conference protects Polish interests, the Polish people will get drunk beyond reason and will start having bloody pogroms!'

In a large Polish city, a mayor was elected who was known for his hatred of the Jews. Several prominent Jews were invited to the mayor's inaugural ball, and at the end of the evening the mayor thanked his guests for the honour they had shown him by attending. To the Jews he directed a few extra words: 'You Jews demonstrated your dancing skills originally in the desert when you danced around the Golden Calf.'

To this one of the Jewish guests replied, 'You're absolutely right, Sir. We're used to dancing when presented with a beast!'

The Iron Chancellor, von Bismarck, was absolutely fascinated by the acumen of the Jewish politician Eduard Lasker. One day Bismarck said to him, 'Herr Lasker, I want you to have a ministerial post in my cabinet!' To this Lasker replied, 'Herr Chancellor, that won't be possible. This part of my career was cut off when I was eight days old!'

In 1932 the writer Israel Zangwill travelled from London to Berlin to take part in a Zionist meeting. In Berlin he went into a cafe and seated himself at the only vacant place, next to two women. When the women saw Zangwill reading a Jewish newspaper, one of them said, 'Is there nowhere a German can go without having to meet a Jew?' Zangwill's dry response was, 'Why don't you try hell?!'

After a long meeting in Berlin Israel Zangwill caught a tram. He was so fatigued that he could not suppress his yawns. The woman sitting opposite him was so disturbed by this that she said in an irritated tone, 'Your mouth is so wide open – do you want to swallow me?'

'No, Madam,' Zangwill quickly replied, 'fortunately our religion forbids us a certain type of meat!'

In Czarist Russia a Jewish girl was introduced to the Minister of Culture. He took the silver crucifix from his neck and demanded of the girl, 'Kiss your groom!'

The girl replied with alacrity, 'In a civilized society it is usual for the groom to kiss the bride first!'

✡

During the last years of Czar Nicholas II, a Jew fell into the Moskva River and was in danger of drowning. 'Help! Help! I can't swim!' he cried – but in vain. A group of soldiers sitting idly by just laughed and did nothing.

In his despair the Jew had a life-saving idea. He started crying: 'Down with the Czar! Long live the Revolution!'

Immediately the soldiers jumped into the river, pulled the man ashore and took him to prison, saying, 'That'll teach you to insult our Czar!'

✡

Tristan Bernard, the famous Jewish humorist, took his seat in a train compartment reserved for non-smokers and lit a cigarette. The only other occupant of the compartment complained, but to no avail. Bernard carried on smoking, completely unmoved.

The non-smoker called the guard. When the guard drew Bernard's attention to the non-smoking notice, the humorist said, 'Instead of rebuking me for my smoking you'd be better employed showing this other gentleman into a second-class compartment, because this is a first-class one!'

The guard demanded to see the other passenger's ticket and, indeed, it was only second class. The man had to leave Bernard's compartment.

On telling this story to a friend, Bernard was asked how he knew that the other man was in the wrong compartment.

'Quite simple,' said Bernard. 'I saw that his ticket was the same colour as mine!'

✡

'Tell me, Klaus-Wilhelm,' said one German student to another, 'why are you against the admission of Jews to the student fraternity?'

'Because those fellows study too much and drink too little – they aren't real students!'

✡

A teacher in a German private school rebuked her only Jewish pupil: 'You're just the same as all the rest of your race – selfish, greedy and arrogant. Your father pays the fees for one pupil, and what are you doing? Learning enough for three or four!'

✡

The great Jewish comic Groucho Marx (1895–1977) was trying to gain admission for his son to an exclusive swimming club which did not allow Jews to be members. When his application was refused for the third time, he said to the club chairman, 'OK, your rules don't

17

allow the admission of Jews. But my son is a half-Jew.
May he dive into your pool up to his waist?'

✡

A Heidelberg society lady arranged for a dance party
in her villa. At the last minute she realized that
some gentlemen had declined her invitation and so she
was lacking seven male dancing partners. At that time
Heidelberg had an American garrison, so she phoned the
barracks and said to the commanding officer, 'Please
send me seven officers who can dance with ladies, but
please, no Jews.'

'That'll be no problem, Madam,' said the
commanding officer. At seven o'clock sharp seven
officers duly arrived at the villa – all of them were black!
The lady of the house, totally confused, stuttered: 'There
must be some mistake!'

'I'm afraid not, ma'am,' said one of the officers.
'Colonel Bloomfield never makes a mistake!'

4
THE ASSIMILATION

During the Assimilation, which was advocated in Germany by Moses Mendelssohn (1729–86), many Jews were baptized as Christians in the hope that this would enable them to achieve a quicker and more thorough integration into Christian society. Against this background many jokes were told about the efforts of those Jews who used any and every means to ingratiate themselves with their non-Jewish neighbours.

Jankel Goldstein from Lemberg wanted to pursue his career in Vienna, and so decided to get baptized to make matters easier. The evening before his baptism he asked a Christian colleague what he should wear for the occasion. His colleague replied, 'We usually go in nappies!'

✡

Moishe and Schmuel had heard that the Catholic pastor gave 100 crowns to everyone who was to be baptized. They decided that Moishe would receive baptism and would share 100 crowns with Schmuel. When the freshly baptized Moishe came out of church, Schmuel greeted him with an open palm. Moishe looked down on him with contempt and said, 'That's exactly why we Christians don't like you Jews – all you think about is money!'

✡

A Jew received a Protestant baptism. When the pastor asked him what name he wanted as a Christian, he replied, 'If I may, I would like to choose the name Martin Luther.'

The pastor said, 'Of course you may, but why do you want to be called Martin Luther?'

The newly baptized man answered, 'Well, you see, all my clothes have been embroidered with my old name, Moishe Levy, and it would be a real shame if all the initials had to be re-embroidered!'

✡

Professor Chwolson, a baptized Jew, was asked why he had been baptized. He replied, 'Out of conviction.'

'What do you mean?' he was asked.

'Out of conviction that it's more profitable to be a professor at the University of St Petersburg than to be a Melamed [a teacher of children] in Schklow!'

✡

A schoolboy named David Cohen brought his end-of-term report home to his parents. His father noted that his marks had become even worse than last term's. 'There must be a reason why you get such bad marks,' said his father. 'Don't you do your homework? Don't you learn?'

'Oh yes,' replied the boy, 'but the teacher can't stand Jews, so he gives me bad marks because I'm a Jew!'

The father wanted to spare his son further trouble, so he had him baptized. The boy was given a Christian name: now he was no longer David Cohen but Irving Collins. Nevertheless, at the end of the next term Irving Collins had even worse marks than David Cohen.

'What excuse do you have this time?' asked his furious father. 'You can't tell me that your teacher still has prejudice against you!'

'No, that's true,' said the boy, 'but all the other children in the class are Jewish, and you can't compete with Jews!'

Moshe Levy from Warsaw, who had become quite wealthy, decided to give his only daughter the best possible education, and so sent her to an exclusive boarding school in the French-speaking part of Switzerland. After her return to Warsaw she got married, and a year later she went into hospital to give birth to her first baby. The father waited nervously in the next room. Then he heard a cry from the maternity ward: *'Mon Dieu! Mon Dieu!'*

'Doctor!' called the father. 'Come quickly – the baby will soon be born!'

The doctor, a friend of the family, said, 'Don't panic. There's still time.'

After another hour, a further cry was heard from the maternity ward: *'Oy! Gewalt! Mame, mame!'*

Then the doctor said to the father, 'Now the baby will arrive!'

Samuel Mendelssohn converted to Christianity in order to be admitted to a country club which didn't accept Jews as members. When he introduced himself at the club he was asked, 'What's your name?'

'Seymour Hutchinson.'

'What's your profession?'

'I'm a member of the New York Stock Exchange.'

'A last question: what is your religion?'

'Religion? Er...Goyish!'[1]

Sandy and Samuel, both art lovers, went to the Museum of Ancient Art. They took their old father with them, as he had never been to an art exhibition before. In front of a huge painting depicting the birth of Jesus they said to their father, 'The museum paid three quarters of a million dollars for this picture.'

The father contemplated the picture and asked, 'Is that a family?'

'Yes,' said one son, 'father, mother and baby.'

'And why are they in a stable?'

'Because they were desperately poor and had no money to rent a flat.'

'I see...They were desperately poor, but they could find the money to pay this expensive painter!'

A young man named Jankel went to Warsaw to study at university. His mother was worried that he might forget about his daily morning prayers and his *tefillin*[2] in such a big city. So she decided to put his handkerchiefs in the same bag with his prayerbook and *tefillin*.

Not long after his departure, his parents received their first letter from him, in which he complained that his mother had forgotten to pack his handkerchiefs. His mother wrote back: 'Pray to God and you will find them!'

---

[1]   The word 'Goyish' is derived from *goyim*, meaning 'non-Jewish'.

[2]   i.e. phylacteries, the two small leather boxes containing scrolls from the Torah which Jewish men wear on their left arm and forehead during their daily prayers.

5
RABBIS

An old rabbi had died. In heaven the Archangel Gabriel welcomed him in person and guided him to his place in paradise – an honourable seat in the third row. He took his seat and curiously looked at those in front of him. With some amazement he discovered a man in the first row whom he knew as a bus driver.

'Why is it that a bus driver is sitting in such an honourable place, three rows in front of me?' he asked the Archangel. 'After all, for 40 years I served as a rabbi, and through my sermons I helped people to pray and to live a decent life. Where is the justice in that?'

'We had our reasons,' said the angel. 'You see, when you were preaching, how many people listened and how many fell asleep? On the other hand, that bus driver drove like a maniac at a hundred miles per hour, and his passengers never stopped shaking and praying!'

Three community leaders – a Catholic priest, a Protestant minister and a rabbi – each ordered a gown from the same tailor. When they collected their gowns and asked for their bills the tailor just waved them away dismissively, saying, 'I'm not taking any money from clergymen!'

However, the Catholic priest wanted to show his gratitude, and so sent a silver crucifix to the tailor. The

Protestant minister sent him a leather-bound New Testament. And what did the rabbi send? A colleague!

A rabbi had a serious heart attack and had to spend several weeks in bed. The president of his congregation came to see him and said, 'I have the honour to tell you that at its meeting yesterday the managing board voted to wish you a speedy and full recovery. The motion was passed with a large majority – twelve to seven!'

The priest of a small town in Poland was known for his knowledge of the Bible and the Hebrew language, and he wanted to compete with a nominee from the town's Jewish community in a test of their knowledge of Hebrew.

It was decided that each of the contestants would give his opponent a passage of Hebrew text to translate. If the Jewish representative won, the Jews would be allowed to remain in the town. If the priest won, all the Jews would have to leave.

The rabbi was not prepared to represent the Jews, as he was worried that he might know less Hebrew than the priest. A simple Jewish craftsman volunteered to compete with the priest, and since no other Jew was willing to do it, the Jewish community accepted the craftsman as their representative, although with some anxiety.

After the priest had officially opened the competition, the craftsman asked for permission to go first. Permission was granted, and he asked the priest the meaning of the Hebrew words *Ejneni jodea*, which mean 'I don't know.'

The priest answered, 'I don't know,' upon which the judges declared the craftsman to be the winner. There was great joy and relief amongst the Jews, who had expected the worst. The craftsman was joyfully acclaimed and the leader of the congregation asked him how he came to have the bright idea of using those two words.

The happy man answered, 'I grew up in a village where the rabbi was a fine scholar. One day someone advised me to ask the rabbi about the meaning of the words *Ejneni jodea*. The rabbi answered, "I don't know." So today I thought that if our clever rabbi didn't know what the words meant, then how could the priest know?!'

✡

A new rabbi was appointed to a congregation in which, on each Sabbath, an argument developed about the *Schema Israel* prayer. Half of those praying would remain standing while the other half would sit to pray. Those who stood were convinced that this prayer, which was the last words of Jews burning at the stake, must be spoken while standing. Those who sat said that the *Schulchan Aruch*, the religious law book, allowed everyone who was sitting before the *Schema Israel* to remain seated during it. Those who stood would cry to those who were seated, 'Stand up!' And those who were sitting would cry, 'You should remain seated as well!'

Each Sabbath this argument erupted anew, and so the rabbi decided to finish this dispute once and for all. He knew that in a Jewish old people's home in the city there lived a 95-year-old man who was a founding member of the synagogue. The rabbi went with one representative of each faction to ask the old man what used to happen back in the early days of the synagogue.

The delegation had hardly entered the old man's room when the representative of those who stood asked him, 'Wasn't it the tradition that the *Schema Israel* was said whilst the people were standing?'

The old man answered with a weak but clear 'No.'

'So they remained seated, then?' asked the representative of those who sat.

But the old man again said, 'No.'

Now the rabbi intervened and said to the old man, 'We need a clear statement from you, because each Sabbath one half of the congregation stands and one half sits.'

To this the old man replied, 'That's exactly how it was in my day!'

The rabbi of a local Jewish community was visited by a man who had come from another city. The stranger had brought his ten-year-old son with him. 'My son dreams of becoming a rabbi,' the man explained. 'As we know that you are a shining example of what a rabbi should be like, we have travelled over 100 miles to meet you.'

The rabbi was moved by this. He put his hand on the boy's head and said to him, 'I'm very glad that you intend to become a rabbi – it's a holy vocation. Since you have had such a long journey to meet me, you may ask me any question you wish.'

The boy said, 'Thank you, rabbi. If I may, I would like to ask what else you do apart from preaching?'

'It seems to me,' said the rabbi with a smile, 'that you don't want to become a rabbi, but rather the president of a congregation!'

✡

Two members of a local Jewish community had been having a continuous argument for over two years. On the eve of Yom Kippur the rabbi asked them to come into his office. 'The two of you must be reconciled,' he told them. 'What sense does it make to come to synagogue to ask God for forgiveness of your sins if you're not able to be at peace with your neighbour?'

The two men were moved by his words. They hugged each other and promised that they would never quarrel again.

After the service one of the men said to the other, 'I wish everything to you that you wish to me!'

The other one replied, 'Are you trying to start the argument all over again?'

✡

There is often a difference between what people say and what they mean. For example:

'I don't doubt the sincerity of Mr Stein's statement' really means 'I doubt the sincerity of his statement.'

'Mr Bloom is a tireless member of our managing board' really means 'Mr Bloom is an interfering busybody.'

'My honourable colleague' really means 'To all my enemies I wish such a colleague!'

'I will restrict myself to a few brief remarks' really means 'I'm going to talk for at least an hour!'

✡

A member of one synagogue said to a member of another, 'Our wonderful rabbi talks daily with the Almighty!'

'How do you know?' asked the other man.

'He told me!'

'He might have been lying.'

'Nonsense – the Almighty wouldn't talk daily with a liar!'

✡

Pilpul (a word derived from the Hebrew for 'pepper') is the name of a rabbinic teaching method which is meant to sharpen the brain. A rabbi was once asked by a non-Jewish acquaintance about the meaning of *pilpul*.

'This is best explained by the following question,' answered the rabbi. 'Two chimney sweeps climb up on to a roof to clean a chimney. They slip and fall down the chimney. The face of one is covered in soot while the other remains clean. Which of the two is going to wash his face?'

'The sooty-faced one, of course,' replied the acquaintance.

'No, the exact opposite – the clean one washes his face! As the sooty one sees his colleague's clean face, he believes that he also is clean. The clean one sees the sooty face of his colleague and therefore believes that his face is sooty as well, and that's why he goes to wash!

'Then the two men climb on to the roof once more and again fall down the chimney. Again one is sooty while the other is clean. Who will now wash his face?'

'The clean one?'

'You're wrong again! This time the sooty one goes to wash, because when the clean one washed for the first time, he saw that his hands were clean and that he didn't need to wash. This time he won't repeat his mistake.

'Now they climb on to the roof for the third time and fall down the chimney. Who's going to wash himself now?'

'I'll have to think about that!'

'Perhaps you ought to think also about how it's possible for two men to fall down a chimney with one of them remaining clean. You see, my friend, this is *pilpul*!'

✡

The Chief Rabbi of Vienna, Peretz Chajes, was among the guests at a birthday party in honour of the Emperor Franz Joseph of Austria-Hungary. The Emperor gave each of his guests a cigar, and they all lit up except for Chajes, because it was the Sabbath, and in Judaism it is strictly forbidden to light a fire on the Sabbath.

'Why don't you smoke your cigar?' the Emperor asked Chajes.

The Chief Rabbi replied, 'Because in my opinion it would be utterly lacking in respect to allow a cigar from the Emperor to go up in smoke!'

✡

Rabbi Joseph Cahanemann was the founder of the world-famous Poniwez Yeshiva Talmud school and of several other educational institutes in the Israeli town of Bni-Berak. He travelled several times to South Africa, where he had many friends from his original homeland of Latvia, and from them he requested sponsorship for his educational institutes. When he told one friend of his intention to meet a certain rich Jew to ask for a large sum of money, his friend said, 'You'll be wasting your time. That man is very hostile to orthodox Judaism. As soon as he sees you with your beard and your long robe he'll decide that he won't give you a penny!'

Indeed, when the rabbi visited the rich man, he did nothing to hide his anti-orthodox feelings. 'But don't you want Jewish children to have a good education?' asked the rabbi.

'Oh yes, and I'm quite happy to give you money to build a primary school, but only on the condition that the children can sit in class without covering their heads.'

'And if I accept this condition, are you ready to meet the entire cost of the school?' asked the rabbi.

'I'm happy to build such a school!' answered the man with a smile.

'Agreed!' said the rabbi, and they confirmed the matter with a handshake.

A year later the donor was invited to the grand opening of the new school. The wonderful building had a huge sign at the front: 'THE NEW BNE-BERAK SCHOOL FOR GIRLS'. (The religious duty to cover the head only applies to men and boys!)

✡

In a *shtetl* [1] in Czarist Russia a poor man once found a purse which had been dropped on the street. In it were 500 roubles. In the synagogue he had heard that Reb Hersch, the richest Jew in the *shtetl*, had lost his purse and had promised the honest finder a reward of 50 roubles. So the poor man went to Hersch and gave him the purse and waited for the promised reward.

But after counting the contents, Hersch said, 'I see that you've taken your reward already.'

'What do you mean?' demanded the poor man.

'Very simple – in my purse there were 550 roubles.'

'That's a lie! I swear that in that purse there were only 500 roubles! Let's go to the rabbi – he'll find out the truth!'

So they went to the rabbi and they each told their version of events. Hersch said to the rabbi, 'I do hope you believe me and not this beggar!'

'Yes,' said the rabbi, 'I believe that you're telling the truth.'

The poor man was confused. Why did the rabbi so readily believe the rich man?

But then the rabbi took the purse and handed it to the poor man.

'What are you doing, rabbi?' demanded Hersch. 'You just said that you believe me!'

'I do!' answered the rabbi. 'I believe that your purse contained 550 roubles. On the other hand, it seems to me that this poor man is also telling the truth when he says that the purse which he found contained only 500 roubles. If he wasn't an honest man he could have kept all the money for himself. Therefore, I think he hasn't found your purse, but the purse of another man which only contained 500 roubles. Now he must wait until the loser of this purse comes to claim it. In the meantime he may keep it!'

'And what about the money that I've lost?' cried Hersch.

'You'll have to wait until someone appears who has found a purse containing 550 roubles!'

A rabbi was visited by a Jew who offered to give £1,000 to the synagogue if the rabbi would promise to call him up as the Cohen² to do the Torah reading. The rabbi explained that such a thing was impossible.

'In that case,' persisted the man, 'I'll give £5,000!'

'No!'

'£10,000!'

'Impossible!'

'£20,000!'

'You must understand that this can't be bought with money,' said the exasperated rabbi. 'Anyway, why are you so keen to be called up as Cohen for the Torah reading?'

'To tell you the truth, both my grandfather and my father were called up as Cohen, and so I regard it as a matter of honour to be called as Cohen as well.'

✡

'If only I had two more members of the congregational board like you I would consider myself a lucky man!' said a rabbi to one of his most embittered opponents.

'What are you talking about?' replied the man. 'I'm constantly criticizing you! So why would you consider yourself lucky if you had two more people like me?'

'It's quite simple: if I only had two more of your sort I would be lucky – the problem is, I've got another 30 like you!'

¹ A small Jewish village or town.
² A Hebrew priest. The joke here is that since 'Cohen' is an hereditary title, the man was already a Cohen because his father was one, and so he had no need to pay for the title.

6
MATCH-MAKING AND MARRIED LIFE

All peoples make jokes about marriage, and the Jews are no exception. Jewish marriage jokes have some unique themes which stem from the Jewish way of life and folklore. One of these is the Schadchen *or 'match-maker'. The* Schadchen *used to play a decisive role in most Jewish betrothals in Eastern and Middle Europe until the beginning of this century, and is still common today in orthodox Jewry all over the world.*

✡

The *Schadchen* and the future groom were about to make their first visit to the family of the bride-to-be. Knowing the boastful manner of the young man, the *Schadchen* warned him, 'I know you tend to exaggerate a bit. Now listen: if you tell a story and I get the feeling that you're overdoing it, I'll kick you, and then you must say only half of what you originally wanted to say.'

They sat down at the table with the bride and her parents, and the young man began to tell his stories: 'Not long ago I was out fishing, and I caught a pike that weighed...' At this moment he felt a vigorous kick in the shin, and then he continued: '...that weighed at least 100 pounds!'

The family received his story with some amusement and head-shaking.

THE HARPERCOLLINS BOOK OF JEWISH HUMOUR

On their way home the *Schadchen* strongly reproached the young man: 'Didn't we agree that if I kicked you, you would curb your imagination?'

'So what's the problem?' replied the young man. 'The 100 pounds was only half of what I originally wanted to say!'

✡

A young man asked the *Schadchen* how big a dowry a particular girl would get from her father. 'For each year of her life her father will give 1,000 roubles,' replied the *Schadchen*.

'And how old is she?' asked the young man.

'Twenty.'

The young man thought for a moment. 'H'mm. I'm afraid she's too young for me!'

✡

An American tourist put an advertisement in the Israeli press, saying that he was looking for the right match for each of his three daughters. An Israeli young man telephoned the American at his hotel in Tel Aviv and enquired about the age of the daughters.

'My youngest is 20 and gets $20,000 as her dowry,' replied the father. 'The second oldest is 30 and gets $30,000. The third one is 40 and gets $40,000.'

After a moment's thought the young man asked, 'Do you have a daughter who is 50 years old?'

✡

An angry young man challenged the *Schadchen*: 'How dare you offer that girl Rivkah to me as a bride? She's deaf!'

'But that's a great advantage, young man: you can shout at her as much as you like, and she won't hear a thing!'

'But she stutters too!'

'That's another advantage: she won't talk much!'

'But she's ugly!'

'Yet another advantage: she won't flirt around!'

'But she's also ten years older than me!'

'My dear young man, I'm afraid you'll have to put up with one disadvantage!'

✡

A *Schadchen* visited one of his clients to tell him about a girl he had seen on his behalf. 'She's a splendid match for you,' he reported. 'She's young, pretty and rich! She has only one tiny fault: she stutters.'

The young man gave a sign of refusal, but the *Schadchen* quickly retorted, 'But she won't do it all the time – only when she talks!'

✡

Motel Rosenwasser, a Yeshiva[1] student, was about to meet his future bride Reisele for the first time.

'What am I supposed to tell her?' he asked the *Schadchen*. 'I've never had a conversation with a girl in all my life!'

37

'It's simple,' replied the *Schadchen*. 'You should talk to her about love, about family and about philosophy.'

Motel and Reisele were left alone with each other, and the young man immediately started on the first topic, love: 'Reisele,' he asked, 'do you love *lokschen*?'[2]

'No, I don't love *lokschen*,' she replied.

So much for love! Now Motel broached the subject of the family:

'Reisele, does your brother love *lokschen*?'

'I have no brother,' she answered.

That finished the family as a topic of conversation. Now there was only philosophy left to talk about:

'Reisele, if you had had a brother, would he have loved *lokschen*?'

✡

A *Schadchen* once went to see the famous Russian-Jewish banker Brodzki. 'I've got a splendid match for your daughter!' he said.

'My dear fellow,' replied Brodzki, 'my daughter does not need your assistance to get married!'

'If you hear who I'm talking about you'll surely change your mind!'

'And who are you talking about?'

'The Crown Prince of Russia himself – the son of the Czar!'

The banker was overwhelmed, but he was not sure that he believed the *Schadchen*. 'If you really are capable of making this match, then I agree to it!' he said.

The *Schadchen* rubbed his hands with glee, thinking, 'The first half is done. All I have to do now is to get the consent of the Czar!'

✡

Two newly married men were having a chat.

'I married for love,' said the first one. 'And you – did you marry for love or for money?'

'With me it was a combination of both,' replied the other man.

'What do you mean?'

'It's quite simple: I married for love of money!'

✡

Reisele confided to her mother, 'Moishe has proposed to me.'

The mother heard some doubt in her daughter's voice. 'Don't you like him?' she asked.

'Oh, yes, I think I do — but he's an atheist and doesn't believe in hell!'

'I wouldn't worry about that, my dear. Once you're married he'll believe in it!'

✡

Why is it that the husband is obliged to feed his wife, and not the other way round? Because immediately after the creation had taken place, Eve gave Adam something to eat – an act from which we are still suffering to this day!

✡

The suddenly nervous father of the bride sought the rabbi's advice. 'Rabbi, you must help me!' he said. 'I promised the groom a dowry of 20,000 zlotys, but I've only got 10,000! And now he's threatening not to marry my daughter if I don't put the full amount on the table by tomorrow!'

The rabbi pondered the problem gravely. 'Formally, of course, you have to keep your promise. So I suggest that you put the 10,000 zlotys that you have on the table – but in front of a mirror. Then you can tell the groom, "Here are 10,000 and there (in the mirror) are 10,000. That makes a total of 20,000!"'

The troubled man sighed and said, 'Rabbi, do you think I don't know that trick already? The 10,000 zlotys I have already includes the mirror!'

✡

Motke went into a high-class stationer's shop. 'I want to buy the most expensive fountain-pen that you can show me,' he said to the young lady behind the counter. 'It's for my wife's birthday.'

'That will be a surprise for madam,' said the shop assistant, approving of Motke's choice.

'It certainly will – after all, she's expecting a mink coat!'

✡

A Jewish mother was visited by a friend who enquired about the well-being of her children. 'Oh,' exclaimed the mother, 'my poor Davidele, my unfortunate boy! He married a girl who won't move a finger at home. She stays in bed until noon and won't do a thing. Picture this: my poor son serves her breakfast in bed!

'My daughter, on the other hand, made a lucky match. Her husband, the Lord bless him, is an angel. He won't have her moving a finger at home, he serves her breakfast in bed and insists that she stays there until noon!'

In 1912 a little village in the Ukraine was buzzing with rumours that the dreaded Cossacks were about to attack. Most of the villagers were busy digging holes behind their houses to hide their gold and silver from the Cossacks. A poor man named Jankel was digging too, but his hole was about two metres long. A neighbour who had been watching Jankel's efforts sarcastically asked if he really had so much money that he needed such a big hole. The poor man answered, 'My wife Scheindel is dearer to me than gold!'

On a quiet spring evening a poor man named Jankel had just made himself comfortable in his living-room when a stone crashed through his window and dropped on to the floor. He picked up the stone, around which a shabby piece of paper had been wrapped. He unwrapped it and read the following message: 'If you don't pay us – according to our instructions given below

– £10,000 by tomorrow noon, we'll abduct your wife!'
Jankel took a pen and wrote his answer:

Dear Sir,
Received your stone with letter. At this moment
I do not have £10,000. But please keep in touch.
Your offer interests me.
Yours sincerely
Jankel Goldstein.

Not long ago the following advertisement appeared in a Jewish newspaper:
Businessman is looking on behalf of his daughter
(28 years old, big dowry) for a good-looking, well-to-do
gentleman (30–45), preferably in independent profession.
Contact: M. Friedlander, tobacconist.

On the following day an old, bearded Jew, rather
poorly dressed, asked to see Mr Friedlander.

'What can I do for you?' asked Friedlander.

'Are you the gentleman who is looking on behalf of
his daughter for a gentleman, well off and under 45?'

'Yes, but I'm sure you passed that age a long time ago.'

'That's why I'm here! I thought I ought to let you
know that you can't count on me!'

Jankel and Berl were having one of their frequent
arguments. 'My wife is so intelligent,' began Jankel,
'that she can talk for hours about any odd subject.'

'And my wife is so clever,' answered Berl triumphantly, 'that she doesn't even need a subject to talk for hours!'

✡

A young man went to his rabbi for some advice. 'Rabbi,' he said, 'I've met a girl I like, but now I can't decide whether I should marry her or not. What do you think?'

'Well, I'd say, yes, marry her!'

'But she's so ugly!'

'Well, don't, then.'

'On the other hand, she'll get a huge dowry!'

'Then marry her!'

'But she limps!'

'Well, don't then.'

'On the other hand, her father has promised to help me to build up my own business.'

'Then marry her!'

'But Rabbi, I had hoped you would give me some good advice!'

'All right. Here's one very good piece of advice for you: go and get baptized.'

'But why?'

'Because then you'll get on the vicar's nerves instead of mine!'

✡

A widowed Jew married for a second time, but the marriage didn't work out – the man was utterly unhappy with his second wife. In his sorrow he prayed to

God, 'Almighty, I know a man must not take two women – that is punishable. But this only applies to us human beings – it doesn't apply to you, Lord. And so I ask that just as you took my first wife, please take the second one as well!'

✡

Jankel the *schnorrer*[3] had learned a lot about money matters during his long life. One day he asked his neighbour Moishe, 'If you had the choice between six daughters or £6 million, what would you choose?'

'What a stupid question!' replied Moishe. 'I'd have the £6 million, of course!'

'I don't think my question's that stupid,' said Jankel. 'You see, if you had £6 million you would still want more – but with six daughters you would surely have had enough!'

✡

Jankel's mother in law, who had made his life hell, had died. When the undertakers arrived, Jankel asked them to take the funeral procession not through the main street but through a narrow back lane instead. When asked the reason why, Jankel modestly answered, 'I don't want to be envied by the whole town!'

---

[1]   A place where Jewish men study the Torah and the Talmud.
[2]   Noodles.
[3]   The kind of man who is always trying to get something for nothing.

7
MONEY MATTERS

During their summer holidays two friends named Jankel and Jossel met at Miami Beach. Over cocktails they discussed their latest business successes. Jossel said, 'Last year my factory burnt down completely. Fortunately I had over $500,000 worth of insurance cover!'

'That's interesting,' replied Jankel. 'Something quite similar happened to me. My shop was devastated by a hurricane. Fortunately my insurance policy covered me with $1 million.'

'That's fantastic!' exclaimed Jossel. 'Would you mind telling me how you managed to kindle a hurricane?'

✡

A learned Jew complained to his rabbi that people were constantly visiting him, and so he didn't have enough time for his beloved study of the Torah.

'I think I've got a fine answer to your problem,' said the rabbi with a smile. 'If a rich man visits you, ask him for a loan – I'm sure you won't see him again. And if a poor man comes to see you, give him a loan – trust me, you won't see him again either!'

✡

It was one o'clock in the morning, and Jankel was walking up and down in the bedroom. 'What's the matter?' asked his wife sleepily. 'Can't you get to sleep?'

'Our neighbour Shlomo across the road gave me a loan of £1,200, and I must return it to him by tomorrow morning. But I don't have the money, and I don't know what to do about it!'

Jankel's wife leapt out of bed, opened the window and shouted across the road, 'Shlomo! Shlomo!'

Eventually the opposite window was opened and a sleepy man angrily asked, 'What is it?'

'You know my husband owes you £1,200? Well, he hasn't got the money!'

After which she closed the window again and said to her husband, 'Now you can go to bed and sleep and let *him* walk up and down in his bedroom!'

✡

Marcus Goldman, the director of a small bank, met his friend in a cafe. The friend noticed a hint of worry in Goldman's face. 'You're looking so serious today,' he said. 'Do you have any problems?'

'I suppose one could call it a problem,' replied Goldman. 'I'm looking for a cashier.'

'But you hired a cashier only two weeks ago!'

'That's exactly the one I'm looking for!'

✡

A typically Jewish curse: 'May you become a rich man – the only rich man in your family!'

For the first time in his life, Jankel the *schnorrer* was deeply depressed. All his attempts to support his family by honest means had failed. Now he decided to work as a bandit. He hid at the crossroads near his village and waited for his first 'client'.

He didn't have to wait long. Soon a group of Jews approached, and when they were close enough he drew his large knife and shouted 'Hands up!'

They all raised their hands except for an elderly woman.

'Hands up, I said!' cried Jankel furiously.

'I can't raise my hands,' said the old woman in a fragile voice. 'My arms are hurting.'

'What?' said the bandit. 'You've got pain in your arms? Come home with me – I've got some balm that'll ease it.'

✡

Moishe had gone to see the solicitor Rosenblum. 'Sir,' said Moishe, 'you must help me to win my case in court tomorrow!'

'What are the charges?' asked Rosenblum.

'Jankel demands the £500 I borrowed from him last year.'

'Did you give him a bill of exchange?'

'Of course I did.'

'In that case you have to pay, I'm afraid – unless…'

'Unless?'

'Unless you can appear to be so crazy in court that the judge must release you on grounds of diminished responsibility.'

'I see. And how am I going to do that? What should I say to the judge?'

'You must answer his questions in such a stupid way that he has no choice but to release you.'

The following day in court the judge asked Moishe, 'Defendant, did you borrow £500 from the complainant?'

'So what?' replied Moishe.

'Then you have to pay back the £500!' said the judge.

'You don't say!' laughed Moishe.

'You don't seem to have noticed that you are standing before a judge!'

'So what?'

'I can send you to prison for three months for insulting the court!'

'You don't say!'

'This man isn't normal!' said the judge in exasperation. He turned to Moishe: 'You can go, but I don't want to see you in court ever again!'

Moishe, very pleased with himself, was just about to go when his solicitor, who was present during the hearing, approached him and said, 'You see – you followed my advice and you were released!'

'So what?' said Moishe.

'You owe me a fee of £100 for my legal advice.'

'You don't say!' laughed Moishe.

✡

Isaac Lieberman entered Jonathan the watchmaker's shop. 'Jonathan,' he complained, 'two weeks ago you repaired my watch and you promised that it would last until the end of my life – and now it's stopped!'

'Well, you see,' replied Jonathan, 'two weeks ago you were looking very ill…'

✡

For well over a year Moishe had owed Jankel £1,000. He had ignored all four of Jankel's written reminders. Suddenly he decided to send his creditor (who lived in another town) a telegram containing only one word: 'Now?' There was a prompt telegraphic answer: 'Now now!'

✡

Shlomo and Isaac met in the street. 'Tell me, Shlomo,' said Isaac, 'do you know what was wrong with Kaminski? He died so suddenly!'

Shlomo shrugged his shoulders. 'Nobody knows,' he said.

'That's strange,' pondered Isaac. 'While Kaminski was alive nobody knew how he lived, and now nobody knows how he died.'

✡

Moshe ordered a pair of trousers from Chaim the tailor. Chaim promised from the bottom of his heart to get them ready in two weeks' time. But one month went by, and then another month, and yet the trousers were anything but ready. After three months of waiting Moshe lost his patience. He went into the tailor's shop and shouted at him, 'Three months aren't enough for you to make a pair of trousers – while the Almighty, blessed be he, created the whole world in six days!' To which Chaim, unmoved, replied, 'And doesn't it look like it!'

✡

Jankel was once again in need of money. 'Moshe, please, lend me £100!' he said. But Moshe remained silent.

'Moshe, I beg you, lend me £100!' Moshe still didn't answer.

'Moshe, you owe me an answer!'

'I'd rather I owed you an answer than you owed me £100!' said Moshe.

✡

Jack Goldstein visited the Chase Manhattan Bank, where he asked for a loan of $100 for one year.

'Can you offer us any guarantees?' enquired the bank clerk.

Goldstein opened his briefcase and pulled out a thick bundle of securities. 'Will these do?' he asked.

The clerk took a closer look at the papers: they were real 'blue chips' worth at least $50,000! 'That will do nicely, Mr Goldstein,' said the clerk. 'Here is your $100, minus $6 interest per annum. When you repay us the £100 in a year's time you'll receive your securities in return.'

The General Manager, having watched the whole scene from his desk, called to Goldstein and asked him, 'Can you tell me why a man like yourself, who owns securities of at least $50,000, needs a loan of $100?'

'It's quite simple,' replied Goldstein. 'Just show me a bank in New York that offers me a safe for my securities for only $6 per year!'

✡

A schnorrer came to the door of Baron Amschel Rothschild's house. 'His Lordship is not available,' a servant told him.

'Not even for a word?' persisted the schnorrer. 'I promise I'll only say one single word!'

The servant left him at the door and told the Baron about this stubborn visitor. The Baron was curious, and so told the servant to let the schnorrer in.

The schnorrer entered, bowed and said 'Gemara!'

'What does "Gemara" mean?' asked the Baron.

The schnorrer replied, 'Gemara, or G – M – R – A, are the initials of the four words, "Good morning, Rabbi Amschel!"'

The Baron smiled and said, 'Very clever. You can go now!'

But once again the schnorrer said 'Gemara!'

'What does "Gemara" mean now?' asked the Baron.

'Give money, Rabbi Amschel!'

The Baron was amused by this, and so took 500 francs out of his purse and gave them to the schnorrer.

But once again the man said 'Gemara!'

'And what does it mean this time?' demanded the Baron.

'Give more, Rabbi Amschel!'

✡

A poor and very distant relative of Baron Rothschild was invited into the Baron's magnificent villa in Paris. On his return to his own village, his wife asked him if the Baron was really as rich as people said.

'My dear,' the man replied, 'that's all nothing but a fairy tale. I think the Baron isn't really well off at all!'

'My goodness me! Why do you say that?'

'I saw it with my very own eyes: the two daughters of the Baron played the same piano at the same time!'

✡

Two brothers who were relatives of Baron Rothschild used to see him once a year, when they would both receive 1,000 francs. This year, for the first time, only one brother turned up, and the Baron soon learned of the sad passing away of the other brother. On his farewell the visitor received his usual 1,000 francs.

'But where are my brother's 1,000 francs?' he asked.

'But you told me he's dead!' said the puzzled Baron.

'So what? Are you his heir?'

✡

The old Baron Rothschild had died. The funeral cortege was a long one, and the participants remained absolutely silent. Only an elderly, poorly dressed Jew sobbed loudly. A journalist approached the man and said to him, 'You're mourning so deeply for the Baron! Are you a relative?'

'No!'
'So why are you crying so much?'
'Because I'm not a relative!'

The first Baron Rothschild, who had come from a poor family, took a taxi back home from his bank. The meter stopped at 90 francs, and the Baron paid with a 100-francs note, telling the driver to keep the change.

The driver frowned and said, 'I hope you don't mind me saying so, sir, but your son is a lot more generous with his tips than you are!'

'Big deal!' the Baron calmly replied. 'He's got a rich father.'

Each month Jankel the *schnorrer* received a certain amount of money from another Jew. On one of these occasions Jankel's benefactor told him that this month, sadly, he couldn't have the money.

'I've had very high expenses this month,' explained the benefactor. 'My wife fell ill and I had to send her to Karlsbad to take a cure. Now, it's very cold in Karlsbad, you know, so I had to buy her a fur coat.'

'A fur coat?!' exclaimed the *schnorrer*. 'With my money?!'

A *schnorrer*, his wife and their seven children entered a first-class restaurant in Brooklyn. The waiter welcomed them and asked if they wanted a table for nine.

'I've been told that bread and mustard come free in this restaurant,' remarked the *schnorrer*.

'That's correct, sir.'

'Then please bring us nine servings of bread and mustard.'

The waiter was speechless and went and asked his boss what to do about this impertinent customer. 'Don't worry, Jack,' said the boss. 'Leave him to me. I'll deal with him!'

He went to the table, but before he could get a word in, the *schnorrer* asked him, 'Are you the boss?'

'Yes.'

'In that case, would you be so kind as to explain why they aren't playing any music in this restaurant today?'

✡

A *schnorrer* entered an exquisite fish restaurant in London. After being seated, he asked the waiter, 'What can I eat for my money?'

'Here's the menu, sir,' replied the waiter. 'You can order anything that's on it.'

The man ordered a three-course meal. When he had finished it he was presented with a bill for £42. He took £2 out of his pocket and said to the waiter, 'I asked you what I could eat for my money. Well, this £2 is all the money I've got.'

The furious waiter went to his boss and told him the whole story. The boss went to the *schnorrer* and said, 'I won't call the police – that is, if you'll walk across the road, go into my rival's restaurant and play the same trick on him!'

'I'm very sorry,' replied the *schnorrer* with a smile, 'but that's where I was yesterday, and the owner sent me over here!'

A London *schnorrer* had developed heart problems, so he went to see the most expensive specialist in Harley Street. When the specialist presented him with the bill, the *schnorrer* told him that he didn't have a single penny.

The stunned doctor asked, 'Then why on earth did you come to see the most expensive doctor in London?'

'Well, you see,' explained the *schnorrer*, 'for my health nothing is too expensive for me!'

Heinrich Heine (a famous Jewish writer) was once asked why he had converted to Christianity. This was his reply: 'I couldn't get used to the idea of having to share Baron Rothschild's faith without participating in his wealth!'

For some time a peanut seller had been plying his trade right opposite the Rothschild Bank. One day an old friend asked him for a loan. 'You should have come a couple of weeks earlier,' the peanut seller replied. 'If you'd asked me then I would have loaned you the money. Meanwhile I've come to an agreement with the Rothschild Bank: I don't give loans and they don't sell peanuts!'

✡

A *schnorrer* had managed to beg a few shillings from a rich man, who mere minutes later discovered him in a fine restaurant, enjoying a portion of salmon with bagel. The rich man approached him and said, 'So you're using my money to buy yourself salmon and bagel!'

'Look, mister,' the *schnorrer* replied, 'when I have no money, I can't eat salmon and bagel. If I also can't eat it when I do have money, when *can* I eat it?'

✡

Hayim Green wrote a telegram to his brother Joshua, inviting him to his son's wedding. It said: 'Joshua Green, 33 Woodpark Avenue, Manchester. Come tomorrow to my son's wedding! Your brother Hayim.'

When Hayim found out how much it would cost to send this message, he decided to shorten it. 'Come' was unnecessary – after all, why would he send a telegram to his brother? To tell him to stay at home? 'My son's' was unnecessary too, because his brother knew he had only one son.

So all that was left was 'Tomorrow...wedding. Your brother Hayim.' But there was no real need for 'wedding', was there? What else would one expect with a 24-year-old son? Circumcision, perhaps, or the *Barmitzvah*? And he could delete 'tomorrow' too. Would he send a telegram if things weren't urgent? And why 'Your brother Hayim'? After all, his brother knew his name, and he only had one brother!

And the address, 'Joshua Green, Manchester' was, of course, completely unnecessary – for who on earth would send a telegram without any text at all? And so, not without pride, Hayim Green presented a blank form to the telegram clerk...

✡

Jack Rosenthal wants to buy a train ticket. 'Quick, a ticket to Springfield, please – my brother has died!'

'Which Springfield do you want?' asked the ticket clerk. 'Springfield in Ohio, or Springfield in Illinois, or Springfield in Pennsylvania?'

Jack wiped the tears out of his eyes. 'Which is the cheapest of the three?'

✡

Sam made a bet with his friend Moshe that he could eat a portion of blintzes (pancakes) in a restaurant without paying a penny. He went to a restaurant and ordered a portion of latkes (potato pancakes). When the waiter served the latkes, Sam said, 'On second thoughts, I'd rather have blintzes.'

The waiter took the latkes away and returned after a few minutes with a portion of blintzes. Sam enjoyed his meal, got up and was about to leave, when the waiter called to him, 'Excuse me, sir, but you haven't paid for your blintzes yet!'

'But I gave you the latkes in return for the blintzes!'

'But you haven't paid for the latkes either!'

'Why should I? I haven't eaten the latkes!'

✡

Sam and Moshe were invited to a golden wedding celebration, and custom dictated that each guest had to give the couple a gold present. 'Let's think for a moment,' Sam said to Moshe. 'What would be a good present – one that's made of gold and yet won't cost much?'

'Find one yourself,' Moshe replied. 'I'll do the same.'

On the evening of the golden wedding Sam said to the golden couple, 'For your golden wedding I've brought you a golden present,' and he gave to them...a packet of 'Gold Filter' cigarettes! Sam rubbed his hands, utterly pleased with himself and convinced that Moshe wouldn't have thought of a cheaper present.

But he was wrong. Moshe appeared, and with him was another man. He went to the golden couple and said, 'Dear friends, for your golden wedding I bring you my brother-in-law...Mr Goldberg!'

A conductor on a London bus was having an argument with a passenger. The fare was 80 pence, but the man was willing to pay only 40 pence.

'Look mister, 80 pence is the fare,' said the conductor. 'Prices have risen. You'd better pay, or else you'll be in trouble!'

'I'll give you 40 pence,' replied the passenger, 'and not a penny more!'

As the bus was crossing Westminster Bridge, the conductor lost his temper, took the passenger's suitcase and threw it off the bus into the Thames.

'*Oy, gewalt!*' cried the man. 'As if it isn't enough that you're charging usury prices! Now you've even thrown my poor, innocent grandson into the river!'

8
THE NOUVEAUX RICHES

To impress one of his friends, a newly rich Jew bought a Lincoln International car and a Rembrandt. A few hours after making these purchases he phoned his wife:

'Harriet, darling, this morning I bought a Lincoln International and a Rembrandt. Have they been delivered yet?'

'Well, sweetheart,' replied his wife, 'one of them has arrived – I just don't know which one!'

✡

A Jewish couple were on a New York sight-seeing tour. They saw Chinatown, Central Park, the Empire State Building and Fifth Avenue.

'On the right side,' said the guide, 'you see the Villa Vanderbilt.'

'Cornelius Vanderbilt?' asks the husband, trying to impress the other passengers with his general knowledge.

'No, William,' replied the guide. 'And here on the left you see the Villa Astor.'

'John Jacob Astor?' asked the husband.

'No, Vincent. And here on the right you see the famous Christ Church...'

At that moment the wife pulled her husband's sleeve. 'Don't, Seymour, please!' she begged. 'I'm afraid that this time you'll make a real fool of yourself!'

The newly rich Mrs Jacobson of New York asked a language tutor to teach her daughter a foreign language.

'Which language does madam have in mind?' enquired the tutor. 'French, Italian, Spanish or Russian?'

'Well, which of the four is the most foreign?'

Mr and Mrs Levy had just moved home from the East Bronx to the high-class Riverside Drive. In an exclusive furnishing store in 5th Avenue they were trying to find the matching furniture for their new villa. The salesman showed them a bedroom suite: 'This here is a real Louis XIV bedroom!' he said.

Mr Levy was happy with the bedroom, but his wife had her doubts about the width and length of the bed. 'It seems a little too small,' she said to the salesman. 'Couldn't you perhaps show us a Louis XV or even a Louis XVI as well?'

A Jewish mother was walking through Brooklyn with her two children. When a passer-by enquired about the children's age, the mother answered, 'The doctor is three years old and the lawyer is two!'

✡

During her visit to Paris the newly rich Mrs Goldberg wanted to see the famous Opera. At the box office she asked for two tickets.

'For Madame Butterfly?' asked the ticket seller.

'No, for Mr and Mrs Goldberg!'

✡

Mrs Jacobs met a lady whom she hadn't seen for a while. She noticed the lady's mourning dress.

'Have you lost a close relative?' she enquired.

'Yes, my husband recently died,' answered the lady.

'Oh, I'm so sorry! My heartfelt condolences.'

'Thank you.'

'It must be terribly hard to make a living all on your own.'

'Financially I'm all right. My husband left me $1 million.'

'Is that all he owned?'

'Oh no, he left a second million for the funeral!'

'Oy! That must have been some event!'

'Indeed it was. He left a further million for the stone.'

'A million for a stone! What a marvellous stone that must be!'

'Oh, yes, it is!' the lady agreed, showing the 24-carat diamond ring on her finger...

✡

During a gala dinner Albert Einstein had the dubious pleasure of being seated next to a Jewish lady who hadn't got a clue about science, and yet was keen to make clever conversation with the famous physicist.

'Mr Einstein,' she said, 'can you explain to me the difference between time and eternity?'

'Madam,' he answered, 'even if I spent all my time explaining this matter to you, it would take an eternity for you to understand it!'

9
DOCTORS AND PATIENTS

A doctor phoned his patient: 'I'm very sorry, but the cheque with which you paid my fee has come back to me from the bank today!'

'My backache has come back too,' answered the patient. 'It seems we're square!'

As the wife of the highly successful Mr Finkelstein, Rachel tried to impress people with an unusual vocabulary. Asked by her doctor how she felt, she answered, 'The forks (she pointed to her fingers) don't work as well as they used to, and also the plate (she pointed to her heart) has, I fear, a crack.'

'I'm afraid, Madam,' answered the doctor, 'that the whole service is broken!'

One year Israel suffered from an unusually cold January. A man from Tel Aviv went to see his doctor: 'Doctor, I've got a really bad cold, and in three days' time I'm expected to fly to London. Do you know what I can do?'

The doctor pondered the problem and then said, 'Tonight you must sleep on your balcony, stripped naked.'

'Impossible, doctor! I'll surely catch pneumonia!'

'Exactly! You see, there's no proper treatment for a cold, but for pneumonia I've got several treatments!'

✡

Shlomo's wife had been complaining about a sharp pain. When the doctor put a thermometer into her mouth, the woman, a notorious chatterbox, was silent for a few minutes. Schlomo was full of awe: 'Oh doctor,' he said, 'where can I buy such a miraculous instrument?'

✡

A doctor met one of his lady patients in the street, lifted his hat to her and passed by. The patient called out, 'Hello doctor!'

The doctor turned around.

'Doctor, I really don't understand you! How can you pass by me without enquiring how I am?!'

'Well, how are you, then?'

'*Oy!* Don't ask me! Don't ask me!'

✡

A young Jewish orthopaedic surgeon – a beginner yet full of himself – was doing his round through the orthopaedic ward, looking after two patients with shoulder injuries. He checked the first patient, pulled his shoulder and twisted and turned it backwards and forwards until the patient screamed in agony. Then he turned to the second patient and repeated this torture, but this patient didn't even twitch or make the faintest noise.

After the young doctor had left the ward, the first patient turned to the second and said, 'I must say I admire you – but where did you get the courage to endure such torture without a single sigh?'

'Courage? What are you talking about? I didn't use courage – I used my common sense.'

'What do you mean?'

'After I saw what that sadist did to you, I wasn't so stupid as to show him my bad shoulder – I gave him my good shoulder instead!'

✡

Shlomo Green was an Orthodox Jew. When his doctor sent him to hospital for an operation, Shlomo took his *tallit*, his prayer shawl and his *tefillin*. On his first morning there he got up early and bound his *tefillin* around his arm and forehead. An Irish patient, lying next to Shlomo, watched him with increasing interest.

'Ah, it's not for nothing that they're always talking about the clever Jews!' said the Irishman. 'Look at this one: he's hardly been in hospital one day, and already he's measuring his blood pressure all by himself!'

✡

A doctor tried to encourage his patient by telling him, 'You don't have to worry, Mr Epstein, I'm absolutely sure that you'll reach 65 years of age!'

'But doctor, I *am* 65!'

'Well, there you are – I didn't lie to you, did I?'

Moshe Finkelstein was a successful businessman but was notoriously mean. One day, while he was eating fish, a bone got stuck in his throat – he couldn't swallow it or spit it out and he was acutely short of breath. His wife called for the doctor, who managed to remove the bone with a pair of tweezers.

After catching his breath, Finkelstein thanked his doctor gushingly: 'Good man, doctor, good man! Now, how much do I owe you for your two minutes of work?'

The doctor, well familiar with his patient's avarice, replied, 'Finkelstein, I won't tell you a sum – you can just pay me half of what you would have paid when the bone was still in your throat!'

✡

The young Dr Leibowitz had opened his first surgery. It was among the poor people of the New York Lower East Side. One day he visited a desperately poor Jew who had fallen seriously ill. The doctor examined him, prescribed some medicine and left a ten-dollar note on his patient's bedside table.

Early the following morning Dr Leibowitz's phone rang – it was the poor patient wishing to thank his doctor: 'Thanks to your great generosity, doctor,' he said, 'I'm finally able to see a specialist!'

✡

Jacob Rabinowitsch from Russia had saved just enough money to fly to America to see his cousin, who was ill in hospital. Standing by his bedside, Jacob asked his relative what was wrong with him.

'I don't know,' sighed the cousin. 'For each illness the doctors have imaginative names. But all I know is that I've been lying here for two months, and so far it's cost me $800!'

'*Oy, vay!* Back home in Odessa you could be ill for a whole year with that money!'

✡

A Jewish woman had begun labour, and her husband rushed her to hospital. All night long he walked up and down in front of the maternity ward, hearing his wife crying and sobbing with pain. He was almost having a nervous breakdown, but then the doctor came out and told him, 'It's a daughter!'

'Thank heavens for that! She'll never have to suffer what we men go through during labour!'

10
JEWS IN THE ARMY

In 1914, at the start of World War 1, a group of Talmud students in Czarist Russia were called up and sent to the front. Their officer commanded them to fire at the enemy, but not a single shot was fired.

'Fire, I said!' Not a shot.

'Why on earth don't you shoot?' the officer demanded.

One of the students answered, 'Because there are people on the other side who might – heaven forbid! – get hurt!'

During World War 1 Jews were fighting on both sides of the conflict. In the Austrian army, an officer promised a medal to the soldier who would go and capture some enemy troops.

Moishe Goldbaum volunteered. He walked out into no man's land and a little later returned with nine enemy soldiers! When his perplexed officer asked him how he managed that stunt, Moishe explained, 'Pretty simple, sir! I walked to the enemy front line and shouted, "Hey, this is for the Jews among you! It's the anniversary of my father's death today and I need a *Minyan* to sing *Kaddish*!"'[1]

A young Chassid[2] had been called up by the
Czarist army and had to appear before a medical
committee which would declare him fit or unfit. The
young man decided to play crazy to be released from
military duty.

When he entered the interviewing room he did so
on all fours. Then he picked up and read every piece of
paper lying on the floor. When the doctor asked him
what he was looking for down there, the recruit gave no
answer, at which point the doctor decided that the
young man was mad. He wrote out a certificate of
unfitness and gave it to the recruit, who took the note
and said, 'Now I can tell you – this is exactly the slip of
paper I was looking for!'

✡

D uring the Japanese – Russian War, in the most
forward Russian position, twelve Russian soldiers
were in a trench. One of them was a Jew. The officer
briefed his men: 'I've just been told that the nearest
Japanese position is held by twelve soldiers. We're now
going to attack them – each one of you will take on one
man. If we capture the position you'll be entitled to
special leave.'

A Cossack with a huge moustache stepped forward:
'Sir, I volunteer to kill two of the enemy!'

The little Jewish soldier rested his rifle on the ground
and said, 'In that case, I don't think I'm needed any
longer!'

✡

During Napoleon's invasion of Russia, Jankel the teacher was one day walking home from the well, when he saw a company of Russian soldiers approaching it. Now, every Russian Jew knew that to meet a man with a bucket full of water was to be blessed by fortune. On the other hand, to meet a man with an empty bucket was to be dogged by misfortune.

The Jews in Czarist Russia had no reason to love their country; moreover, they had heard that Napoleon was benevolent towards the Jews. Therefore Jankel decided to empty his bucket of water before meeting the Russian soldiers, so that the Czarist army would lose its battle with the French.

When he returned home with his empty bucket and his wife asked him why he hadn't brought any water, he explained to her the military meaning of his action. His wife cried, '*Oy, Gottenyu!* You foolhardy man, how dare you get involved when two of the most powerful nations in the world are having an argument!'

✡

The Vietnam war was raging all around. The Sergeant gathered his men and shouted: 'The time has come for us to attack the Viet Cong! It's now man against man!'

Private Silverman raised his hand. 'What?' asked the Sergeant.

Silverman said, 'Did you say it was man against man?'

'Yes! Is there something wrong with your ears?'

'In that case, Sarge, would you please point out to me

the man I'm supposed to fight, as I'm sure that the two of us can sort out our problems amicably!'

✡

During the Allied invasion of Europe in World War 2, an American Jewish soldier saved the life of the Supreme Allied Commander, General Eisenhower.

'You're a very brave young man,' said the General with great feeling. 'If I can do anything for you, let me know.'

'Thank you, sir,' replied the soldier. 'I'd be most grateful if you'd post me to another battalion.'

'Why do you ask that?'

'Because my Sergeant doesn't like Jews.'

'Good grief!' exclaimed Eisenhower. 'You could have asked me to promote you to sergeant – why didn't you do that?'

'Well, sir, the problem is,' explained the private, 'the Sergeant doesn't like Jewish privates, the Lieutenant doesn't like Jewish sergeants, the Captain doesn't like Jewish lieutenants, the Major doesn't like Jewish captains, the Lieutenant Colonel doesn't like Jewish majors, the Colonel doesn't like...Please, General, why don't you do as I ask and move me to another battalion?'

✡

A group of Talmud students were standing at the railway station of a small town in Czarist Russia, when two military trains pulled into the station from opposite directions. In one train were soldiers with grey trousers and in the other were soldiers with red trousers.

'The soldiers with grey trousers are being posted from Warsaw to Moscow,' explained one of the students, 'while those with the red trousers are being sent from Moscow to Warsaw.'

'I don't understand why the Czar makes matters so complicated,' said another student. 'Why doesn't he simply transfer the trousers – the red ones to Warsaw, the grey ones to Moscow – while the soldiers stay where they are?'

'Don't be so silly!' replied the first student. 'If they did as you propose, what would the soldiers wear while their trousers were being transferred?'

✡

During the Vietnam War, an officer was training a group of recruits in the tactics of attack and defence. After discussing different types of emergency situations in which they might find themselves, the officer asked Private Caplin, 'Suppose you are alone in the jungle and a Viet Cong guerilla jumps out of hiding with a huge knife in his hand. What steps would you take?'

'Huge steps, sir – very huge steps!'

✡

During World War I a young Russian Jewish recruit deserted from his unit. He was captured and brought before his Colonel.

'You are a coward and a traitor!' said the Colonel. 'You have brought shame on your country!'

'Sir, I didn't intend to shame my country – I only ran away because I hate the enemy so much that I can't stand the sight of them!'

---

[1] On the anniversary of his parents' death it is a Jew's duty to say a prayer for them in the presence of ten men. A *Minyan* (literally 'number') is ten men, the minimum number required for a religious service. A *Kaddish* is a mourner's prayer.

[2] A member of the Chasidic movement, i.e. a very pious Jewish man.

*However tragic the situation, the Jew will always find
a humorous side to it. Even during the Nazi era, a time
when Jews were systematically persecuted, there still
was the strength to tell a joke, thereby wresting a smile
from an otherwise desolate existence.*

*A*pril 1935. A Jew was sitting on a park bench in Berlin
reading *Der Stürmer*, the Nazis' agitation newspaper.
Another Jew passed by and said to him, 'How a Jew
can read such a mean, anti-Semitic paper I don't know!'

The other answered, 'Look, if I read the Jewish press it
breaks my heart – because what am I going to read there?
Here Jews were abused, there they lost their jobs and
somewhere else they were put in prison. You see, that's
why I'd rather read *Der Stürmer* – because what am I going
to read here? That Jews are ruling the whole world – the
entire world trade lies in their hands and they influence all
governments. That makes me feel a lot better!'

✡

*M*unich, 1936. Jacob Bloom was carrying a chicken
under his arm on his way to market. An SS soldier
stopped him and demanded, 'Jew, what are you doing
with this chicken?'

'I'm on my way to the market to buy food for it.'

'What food?'

'Wheat grain.'

'Grain?! German women are starving, and you Jews are feeding your chickens with grain!' He hit Bloom hard in the face.

Bloom moved on, but then a second Nazi barred his way. 'Where are you going with that chicken?'

'To the market to buy some food for it.'

'What does it eat?'

'Wheat grain.'

'What?! Wheat! The Jews are feeding their chickens with wheat while our children are starving!' He knocked Bloom to the ground. The poor man was hardly back on his feet when a third Nazi arrived.

'Where are you going, Jew?'

'To the market to buy some food for my chicken.'

'What does it eat?'

'I'm not quite sure. I think the best thing is to give it two marks and then it can choose its food for itself!'

✡

What does a real Aryan look like? Blond, like Hitler; slim, like Goering; and athletic, like Goebbels!

✡

Joseph Goebbels, Hitler's Propaganda Minister, was visiting German schools to make sure that the children had absorbed Nazi dogma. In one primary school he encouraged the children to recite patriotic slogans.

'*Heil Hitler!*' shouted one child.

'Very good,' said Goebbels.

'Germany above all!' said another.

'Fantastic!' said the enthusiastic Goebbels. 'What else do you know?'

A boy put up his hand and said, 'May our people live for ever!'

'That's absolutely marvellous! What's your name, young man?'

'Israel Goldberg!'

✡

Berlin, *1936*. One day on the Kurfürstendam, Goebbels grabbed the first Jew he came across and hung around his neck a huge poster saying 'Jews out, Aryans in'. Goebbels ordered the Jew to wear the poster for the whole day in a public place. During the afternoon Goebbels went to check that the Jew was obeying his order. He looked for him all over Berlin and finally found him in a cemetery – with the huge poster around his neck saying 'Jews out, Aryans in'!

✡

One evening a Nazi judge arrived at his club looking very depressed.

'What's the matter with you?' a colleague asked.

'I had a very difficult case today. A Nazi Party member stole 1,000 Reichsmarks from a Jew, and I was forced to sentence him to a whole day in prison.'

'That isn't too bad,' his colleague said. 'After all, you had to maintain the appearance of justice.'

'Oh, it's not the one-day sentence that depresses me, but rather the fact that I had to sentence the Jew to five years in a concentration camp for tempting the poor Aryan with all that money!'

✡

Berlin, 1935. An Aryan boarded a tram and saw that the only free seat was next to a Jew, but on this seat there lay a huge parcel.

'Remove that parcel!' demanded the Aryan.

'Why?'

'Remove that parcel right now, or else I'll call the conductor!'

'Call whoever you like!'

The conductor, a vicious Nazi, shouted at the Jew, 'You will immediately remove that parcel, or I'll throw it out of the window!'

The Jew remained unmoved. The conductor took the parcel and threw it through the open window into the street and shouted, 'That'll teach you to respect other people's rights!'

'It wasn't my parcel!' said the Jew.

*B*erlin, 1937. A tiger had broken out of Berlin Zoo and was rampaging around the city. People were panicking, but a brave young Jew succeeded in recapturing the tiger with a lasso. He restrained it until a keeper could return it to the Zoo.

A newspaper reporter gave the story to his editor, the notorious Jew-baiter Julius Streicher, who published it in *Der Stürmer* under the title, 'Cruel Jew Attacks Helpless Cat'.

*A*dolf Cohen went to the Berlin court to change his name. The judge dealing with his application shouted at him, 'So is this one of your Jewish tricks, then – hiding your Jewish blood behind an Aryan name? Get out of here! Your name is Cohen and will always remain Cohen!'

'But your Honour, I'm most happy with the name Cohen. Please, what I would like to change is my first name, from Adolf to Abraham!'

Two judges were discussing the possible reasons why their courts were always empty. 'I hardly have one trial a month,' the first one sighed. 'I don't understand it.'

'I think I know why,' said the other. 'We have nothing to do because no Jew accuses another Jew, and they wouldn't dare accuse an Aryan. An Aryan, on the other hand, won't accuse a Jew, because that would reveal him as a man who is dealing with Jews.'

The first judge said, 'I think you may have a point there, but surely an Aryan could accuse another Aryan? Why doesn't that happen?'

'That wouldn't work either. Where would he get a Jewish lawyer to handle his case?'

✡

November 1938. Following the Kristallnacht,[1] Samuel Goldberg was sent to Dachau Concentration Camp. In her first letter to him, his wife complained that she couldn't sow her seed-potatoes because she didn't have the strength to dig the vegetable garden.

In his answer, Goldberg wrote, 'Don't you dare dig the garden – that's where I've hidden the guns and ammunition!'

Some days later two lorries full of Gestapo men arrived, equipped with spades, at Mrs Goldberg's home. They stormed into the garden, turned over every inch of earth and, when they couldn't find any guns or ammunition, they left again.

In the next letter to her husband, Mrs Goldberg wrote about this event. His answer was: 'Now, my love, you can sow the potatoes.'

Soon after the war a German Jew, who had miraculously survived the Nazi camps, died from the effects of his suffering. On his way to Paradise, he passed the entrance to Hell. He asked his accompanying angel to show him that part of Hell where Adolf Hitler was to be found. To his surprise, Hitler was sitting in a cell at a desk and was writing.

'Is that the Hell that has been chosen for such a monster?' cried the Jew.

'Calm down, my friend,' said the angel. 'You need not envy him. He has to translate his book *Mein Kampf* into Hebrew!'

Nazi Germany, 1938. Baruch Goldstein was trying in vain to obtain a permit to emigrate to England, where several of his friends were already living.

'It's all Moses' fault,' he said to one of his friends.

'Why Moses?'

'Quite simple. Had Moses not got us out of Egypt in the first place, I would have a British passport today!'²

A Berlin Jew went to a travel agency and asked to see a world map. He began to ponder: 'The United States have closed their gates, Palestine is barred to Jews, England won't let in any more, the South American states are not issuing any more visas…'

In desperation he turned to the travel agent and said, 'Excuse my asking, but do you have another world map?'

✡

In Berlin a Jew accidentally bumped into an SS man. The Nazi shouted 'Pig!' The Jew bowed and said 'Bloomfield.'

✡

Shortly before Nazi Germany attacked Poland and thereby started World War 2, a German delegation led by Finance Minister Hjalmar Schacht arrived in London. Among others, they visited Lord Rothschild, and asked him for a loan for the Third Reich. Of course, Schacht knew that Rothschild was a Jew, yet he believed that he could persuade him to grant the loan by offering favourable conditions.

'I can assure you, my Lord, that we will repay the loan punctually – including interest! We own huge assets. Under the earth we have great coal and iron reserves, and above the earth we have our great Hitler!'

Lord Rothschild looked at him keenly and said, 'I would consider such a request more favourably if your guarantees were the other way round – coal and iron above the earth and...'

*M*ay 1945. At the University of Hanover the Professor of Modern History asked his students for the reasons, in their opinion, for Germany's military defeat.

'It was the fault of the Jews,' said one student. 'There were too many Jewish generals.'

'But there wasn't a single Jewish general in the entire Wehrmacht!' said the Professor.

'I'm not talking about the Wehrmacht – I'm talking about the Allies!'

---

[1] 'The night of broken glass', during which the Nazi militias in Germany and Austria mounted a systematic attack on the Jews and their property.

[2] In 1938 Egypt was still a British Protectorate.

1 2
THE SOVIET UNION

Even under Stalin's iron dictatorship, the Jewish
population of the Soviet Union told jokes which
ridiculed the hated Communist regime and revealed the
allegedly non-existent anti-Semitism.

Molotov was walking through a park in Moscow
when he met a Jew. 'How are you doing in our
Soviet Union?' he asked.

'Thank God!'

'"Thank God?" In the Soviet Union one doesn't say
"Thank God!" but "Thank Stalin"!'

'But Stalin is only a human being,' said the Jew.
'When he dies, what will one say then?'

'Well,' said Molotov, 'then one will say, "Thank
God!"'

✡

In front of a small grocer's shop in Moscow people had
been queuing since five o'clock that morning. They
were waiting for the butter ration which was supposed
to be distributed that day. At seven o'clock the
shopkeeper opened the doors and said, 'I'm sorry, but I'll
receive only half of the promised delivery. There won't
be enough for all. The Jews must go!'

The few Jews waiting in the queue walked away.
The other Russians kept on waiting patiently until four
o'clock in the afternoon. The shopkeeper again opened

the door and said, 'I'm very sorry, but I've just received a phone call – there won't be any butter delivered today. You can all go home.'

A man in the crowd said, 'Strange, isn't it, that the Jews are always treated better!'

✡

A Moscow Jew had bought a parrot and had trained it to say, 'Down with Stalin! Down with the Soviet Union!' Of course, he kept all the windows and doors firmly closed when the bird was talking. One day the Jew had to travel to the Crimea, and he decided to lock the parrot in the fridge so that his neighbours wouldn't hear the slogans. When, after two weeks, the man returned, he took the parrot out of the fridge, and the bird started crying, 'Long live Stalin! Long live the Soviet Union!' The Jew looked at the parrot in puzzlement and said, 'Strange how two weeks in Siberia can change everything!'

✡

R ussia, 1917. The Revolution had been a success: the Communists were in power. Now the farmers had to be convinced that it was better for them to share their land and livestock. The Party Secretary in Kiev visited a farmer and explained the new situation to him.

'Suppose you owned a hundred cows. You would be allowed to keep two of them, and the others would be distributed among the people.'

'Agreed!' said the farmer.

'The same if you had a hundred horses.'

'Agreed!'

'The same again if you had a hundred chickens.'

'No – not chickens!'

'Why?'

'Because I *have* chickens!'

✡

When the Russian Revolution started in 1917 and the Communists took power, the Communists in France believed that their time had also come. A young Jewish Communist walked into the office of Baron Rothschild in Paris and shouted, 'Mr Rothschild, the age of capitalism is over! You'll have to distribute your entire wealth amongst the people!'

Baron Rothschild asked calmly, 'In your opinion, young man, how much is that?'

'At least fifty million francs!'

'And how many people live in this country?'

'Fifty million.'

'That means one franc per person. I'll tell you what, young man. You take your franc and tell each Frenchman to come to me and collect his franc for himself!'

✡

A Moscow Jew who was visiting his nephew in Paris was puzzled about the way of life in the French capital. He asked his nephew, 'Is it true that anyone can change his address, just like that, without any permission from the authorities?'

'Of course one can.'

'And can you change your employer without permission?'

'That's right.'

'And can you even buy a car without permission, just like that?'

'Yes.'

'I really don't understand how you can live in such chaos!'

✡

Brezhnev was visiting Kiev, the capital of the Ukraine. A Jewish delegation approached him. 'Comrade Brezhnev,' they said, 'there are 300,000 Jews in Kiev. Why is it that there is no rabbi in our city?'

'It's not our fault,' answered Brezhnev. 'We had three candidates for the post, but we couldn't accept any of them.'

'Why?'

'Well, the first one had finished his studies at the Rabbinical Seminary in Budapest, but he wasn't a member of the Communist Party. The second was a Party member but hadn't yet finished his studies.'

'And the third?'

'Well, yes, the third was a Party member and he had also finished his studies, but he was a Jew!'

✡

Joseph Abramovitch, a loyal member of the Moscow Communist Party, had a problem. 'My wife is expecting a child at any minute,' he explained to his brother-in-law, 'and the doctor says it'll be a boy.'

'And what's your problem?'

'You must see it from my point of view. As a Communist I can't let my boy be circumcised but, on the other hand, I don't want him to grow up as a *Goy*.' What shall I do?'

Minutes later his brother-in-law accompanied him to the hospital. Joseph went upstairs to the maternity ward while his brother-in-law waited in the hospital entrance hall. Half an hour later Joseph returned, overjoyed.

'It's a girl, thank God!' he announced.

'What do you mean, "thank God"?' said his brother-in-law. 'You Communists don't believe in God.'

'Brother,' said Joseph, 'in this case one has to admit that there is a God. Not only does he demand circumcision, but he's also on the side of the Communist Party!'

Stalin had read in the Bible that in the Messianic time the lion would live peacefully with the lamb. He decided to make this actually happen in order to prove that Communism had brought salvation already. So he ordered the director of the Moscow Zoo to provide a cage in which a lamb and a lion could live together. Of course, Stalin's order was immediately carried out, and the entire foreign press corps was invited to witness the Messianic miracle with their own eyes.

A sceptical BBC journalist asked the director how he had achieved this supernatural miracle.

The director answered, 'It's quite simple – each day we provide a new lamb.'

During the Stalin era a Ukrainian and a Jew were sentenced to death for counter-revolutionary activities. The executioner asked both of them for their last wish.

'I want to smoke a pipe,' said the Ukrainian.

'Agreed. And where do you want to be buried?'

'Next to Alexander Pushkin, our beloved poet.'

'Agreed. And you, Jew – what's your last wish?'

'I want to eat some strawberries.'

'Strawberries?! But there aren't any strawberries in January!'

'Oh, I'm happy to wait!'

'And where do you want to be buried?'

'Next to our great Joseph Stalin.'

'But he's still alive!'

'Oh, I'm happy to wait!'

Stalin had summoned the leaders of the three religions: the Patriarch of the Russian Orthodox Church, the Imam of the Islamic community and the Chief Rabbi of Moscow. Stalin urged them to announce during their next sermons that Communism already existed at the very beginning of human history.

The Patriarch and the Imam indignantly refused. They could not possibly promote such a lie. The Chief Rabbi, on the other hand, accepted Stalin's demand without hesitation.

When his colleagues stared at him in disbelief, he said, 'But Stalin is right. Let us take, for example, the book of Genesis. What do we find there? Two poor people, Adam and Eve, run around naked and barefoot. They fight over one apple, they denounce each other to the authorities, and the whole thing is called Paradise!'

An American Jew was visiting Moscow, where he met another Jew whom he knew from his time as a soldier in the Soviet Army during World War 2. The American asked, 'What are you doing in Moscow?'

'I'm helping to build Socialism!'

'You had four brothers. Where are they now?'

'The first is helping to build Socialism in Warsaw, the second in Budapest and the third in Bucharest.'

'And the fourth?'

'He's in Israel.'

'Helping to build Socialism, I assume!'

'Are you crazy? In our own country?!'

✡

'Is it true,' Jacob asked his friend Mottel, 'that the American constitution guarantees freedom of speech, just like the Soviet constitution?'

'That's absolutely true,' said Mottel, 'but only the American constitution guarantees freedom *after* the speech!'

✡

The Politburo had decided to exclude Jews from the economy. As a result of this, Moshe Rabbinowitz was called to his manager.

'I'm sorry, but we have to dismiss you,' said the manager.

'But why?!' asked Moshe.

'Because you don't have the required qualifications.'

'Give me two months, and I'll get them!'

Indeed, two months later Moshe presented the required certificates to his manager.

'I'm sorry,' said the manager, 'but even so we can't employ you.'

'Why?'

'Your name, comrade, doesn't sound Russian.'

'If that's all, I'll change it immediately!'

Two days later he presented the manager with the certificate of his change of name. Now he was no longer called Moshe Rabbinowitz but Marian Rabanovski.

'You are nevertheless dismissed,' said his manager.

'But why?!'

'Because it gives a bad impression if we only dismiss Jews.'

✡

At three o'clock in the morning a Moscow Jew was woken up by a loud banging on his door.

'Who's there?' he demanded.

'The postman!'

He opened the door and found two KGB agents standing there. They asked him, 'Is your name Jacob Goldstein?'

'Yes.'

'And you have applied for emigration to Israel?'

'Yes.'

'Why do you want to leave the Soviet Union? Don't you have a job?'

'Yes, I do.'

'Don't you have a place to live in?'

'Yes, I do.'

'Don't your children get a good education?'

'Yes, they do.'

'Then why do you want to leave us?'

'Because I don't like living in a country where the post is delivered at three in the morning!'

*M*oscow, *1978*. Goldstein had saved enough money to finally pay for an electric fridge. He went to the appropriate state official and paid him the required amount.

'The fridge will be delivered in exactly ten years' time,' said the official.

'In the morning or in the afternoon?' asked Goldstein.

'What does it matter if it's the morning or the afternoon?'

'Because the plumber has promised to come in the morning!'

In a small Russian village Jankel came home from synagogue and told his wife, 'They say that the Messiah is expected any day now, and then all Jews are going to Israel.'

His wife became hysterical: 'That can't be true! It would be really terrible! It took us years to get our little farm, and now we're expected to just leave it? *Oy, vay!*'

'Don't worry,' her husband reassured her. 'We survived the Pharaohs, we survived Haman and, with God's help, we'll also survive this Messiah!'

✡

Moscow, 10 June 1968. The Six-Day War had just ended in an overwhelming victory for the Israelis. In Moscow, two drunken Ukrainians were in court, charged with beating up two innocent Jews.

'Why did you attack these two Jews? What had they done to you?' asked the judge.

'It was like this,' said one of the accused. 'We'd just emptied a bottle of vodka when we heard on the radio that the Israelis had occupied Gaza. We were quite upset, but we swallowed our anger with more vodka. Then the radio reported that the Israelis were already at the Suez Canal. At that point we grew even more angry, but we swallowed our anger with another bottle of vodka. Then, when we left the bar and walked into the street and saw here, in Moscow, two Jews, we knew what that meant, didn't we? The Jews had advanced this far! At that point we felt we had no choice but to act in self-defence!'

✡

The Khrushchev era. Isaac Aaronowitz had been dismissed from his factory.

'But why?' he asked his boss.

'What did you hold in your right hand during the May Day parade?'

'A picture of Khrushchev.'

'And in your left hand?'

'My dachshund.'

'And what did you get rid of when I ordered you to throw away the dog?'

✡

'In the year 2000 we will land on Venus,' proclaimed Brezhnev in a speech. 'In 2005 we will land on Mars, and in 2010 on Saturn!'

'And when will we be able to go to Paris?' called out Jacob Rabinowitz.

'All in due course,' Brezhnev promptly answered.

✡

'In the year 2000,' said Brezhnev in his May Day speech in Red Square, 'each Soviet family will have its own helicopter!'

'Who needs a helicopter?!' Jacob Rabinowitz asked his neighbour, Moshe Goldman.

'You really haven't got a clue, have you?' replied Moshe. 'Imagine that you live in Kiev and you hear on the radio that in Leningrad they are distributing potatoes. Well, then you take your helicopter and fly to Leningrad!'

✡

A poor woman in a run-down tower block on the edge of Moscow said to her husband, 'What does your Communist regime do for us? Hardly enough to eat, a damp flat and no heating! Why don't you go to your Brezhnev and ask him when we will finally have a decent standard of living?'

So the man asked for an audience with Brezhnev. Two weeks later he was invited to the Kremlin. Brezhnev allowed him plenty of time and even gave him a guided tour of the building. From the window of his luxurious office he showed the man a well-kept park filled with beautiful flowers and said, 'Look at this and remember it well. Tell your wife that in ten years all Russia will look like this!'

The man returned home and told his wife what Brezhnev had said to him. He went to the window, from which he could see the shabby back yard, with its rubbish and stinking dustbins, and children in ragged clothes, and he said, 'You see, my love – in ten years all Russia will look like this!'

✡

A Ukrainian Jew emigrated to Israel, where he was to be met at the airport by his younger brother, whom he had not seen for 50 years. As the 200 passengers were streaming through the terminal building, the younger brother ran towards the older brother and embraced him without any hesitation.

A journalist, having watched this moving scene, approached the younger brother and asked him, 'How did you immediately recognize your brother after 50 years?'

'How did I recognize him? It was quite simple – it was his coat!'

✡

R ed Square, Moscow, May Day 1960. Khrushchev took his place at the tomb of Lenin, and the crowd applauded. Jankel Goldstein cried out enthusiastically, 'Long live Khrushchev!'

Hayim Rabbinowitz, who was standing next to him, said, 'You hypocrite! I can remember very well how you stood here and shouted "Long live Stalin!" and the same for Beria and Malenkov!'

'Well,' said Jankel, 'and do they still live?'

✡

An old Jew was sitting in a Moscow park learning Hebrew. Leonid Brezhnev passed by, saw the Hebrew grammar book and asked the man, 'Why are you learning Hebrew? Do you really think we'll allow you to emigrate to Israel?'

'No, I know you won't, but I'm an old man, and when I die and go to heaven, I want to be able to speak the language.'

'And how do you know you are going to heaven? Perhaps you will go to hell!'

'Well, I'm already fluent in Russian!'

✡

In the Brezhnev era all emigration applications to Israel were denied, with all sorts of excuses. A computer engineer visited the office of the Soviet emigration service and spoke with the Director.

'What is your profession?' asked the Director.

'I'm an electronic engineer.'

'Then you can't emigrate to Israel.'

'Why?'

'Because we don't want you to reveal Russian secrets in capitalist countries.'

'But Comrade Director, you know as well as I do that the electronics technology of the capitalist states is far more advanced than that of our Soviet Union!'

'Exactly – that's the secret they must not know under any circumstances!'

✡

A Jewish journalist from the United States asked a Moscow Jew how he was doing.

'I'm doing badly,' replied the Moscow Jew. 'Why, just today I've been thrown out of the Communist Party for the third time!'

'For the third time?! You must tell me how that happened!'

'It was like this. The first time was after Stalin's death. The Party Secretary told us that the cost of Stalin's funeral was more than one million roubles. I spontaneously said, "So much money for a single funeral? For one million roubles you could have buried the whole Politburo!" So I was thrown out of the Party for the first time.'

'And the second time?'

'That was after Khrushchev's dismissal, when Brezhnev took his place as General Secretary of the Communist Party of the Soviet Union. I was working as a caretaker in the Party offices, and I had the job of changing the two portraits. I was standing there with both pictures in my hand, when the Party Secretary passed by and said, "Come on – throw that dog away!"

I asked him which of the two he meant, and that led to my second expulsion.'

'And what happened today to make them throw you out again?'

'Today the Party Secretary asked me, "Why weren't you at the last Party meeting?" I replied, "Had I known it was the last one, I would definitely have been there!"'

✡

*M*oscow, *1989*. The Factory Director asked his Personnel Manager, 'Why is Abramowitz not at work?'

'He went to the synagogue.'

'What's he doing in the synagogue?'

'He's praying to God for a pay rise. As you know, times have changed, and one is now allowed to pray.'

'I've nothing against praying, but I don't like it when pay rises are decided behind my back!'

✡

I n 1990 it was announced that any Jew who wished to could emigrate to Israel. Moshe Horrowitz arrived at Moscow Airport carrying two suitcases and a long cardboard box. The Russian customs man asked, 'What's that?' pointing to the box.

'You shouldn't ask "What" but "Who"!' Moshe opened the box and took out a heavy bust of Stalin.

'Why do you need this in Israel?' asked the astonished customs man.

'I adore Stalin,' replied Moshe. 'He has defeated

Hitler, he made Russia great, and I want this memento of him in my living room.'

'If you say so,' said the customs man, shrugging his shoulders.

The plane landed at Tel Aviv. The Israeli customs man pointed at the box and asked, 'What's that?'

'Not "What" but "Who"!' Moshe took out the bust of Stalin.

'Why do you need a bust of that monster in Israel?'

'I'll tell you. If I ever have bad times in Israel, all I'll have to do is look at this bust, and I'll stop feeling homesick for the Soviet Union!'

After passing through customs, Moshe met his uncle Aaron, who was going to take him to his little house in Ber-Sheba. After arriving at the house, Moshe opened the box and his uncle saw the bust of Stalin.

'Who's that?' asked his uncle.

'Not "Who" but "What"! This ugly thing is exactly twelve kilos of gold!'

B oris Yeltsin wanted to remove Lenin's corpse from Moscow once and for all. He asked the United Nations to find out if any state would be willing to bury Lenin within its borders.

The only answer came from the Israeli Prime Minister: 'We are willing to bury Lenin in Jerusalem.'

But Yeltsin faxed back: 'Under no circumstances in Jerusalem! There the dead are resurrected!'

---

¹   The Yiddish word *Goy* means 'non-Jew'.

13
THE UNITED STATES

At the beginning of this century, hundreds of thousands of Russian Jews emigrated to America to escape the bloody pogroms. There they found a new home, and gradually, thanks to their hard work and their spirit of enterprise, they established a foothold, and some of them became rich. Their unmistakable Eastern European accents, combined with their often touching attempts to integrate with a not always Jew-loving American society, became the subject matter of countless witty anecdotes.

Moishe Bernstein from Russia had made his fortune in America, and now he had brought his aged father from Russia to New York. After the arrival of the ship, the father hugged his son emotionally and said, 'My beloved son Moishe!'

'Father, please, don't call me Moishe! I'm called Maurice here.'

'Oh, look!' exclaimed the father. 'There's your wife Scheindel!'

'Father, here she isn't called Scheindel but Shirley.'

'But you do keep our traditions, don't you?' asked father. 'And you keep your shop shut on the Sabbath, I hope?'

'Father, we're in America now! Please try to understand!'

'But you do keep kosher, don't you?!'

'Father, this is America!'

The desperate father whispered into his son's ear, 'Moishe, tell me the truth – are you still circumcised?'

✡

Mendel Abramowitz had done everything to become a real Yankee. He now called himself Mark Averall, and his wife Yente was now Jacqui. But he hadn't quite succeeded in entering high society. He sought advice from a Christian friend, who told him to buy a luxurious apartment in Fifth Avenue, to equip it with classical furniture and to buy the work of a famous painter for the lounge. Mark did all of this, spending a lot of money on a real Rubens.

When the non-Jewish guests whom he had invited to the flat-warming didn't turn up, he worried that the name 'Rubens' might sound too Jewish. So he went to the gallery, returned his Rubens and bought a Goya instead![1]

✡

A rich American Jew invited the world-famous violinist David Oistrach to dinner at his villa. 'And don't forget to bring your violin!' he added.

'What for?' asked Oistrach. 'My violin doesn't eat!'

'But surely you'll give us the pleasure of hearing you play it?'

'I see! You're one of those patrons who invites a plumber to dinner, and after the dessert asks him to clear the drain in the bath!'

✡

A rich American Jew told the party organizer whom he had hired to arrange his son's Bar Mitzvah: 'You must think of something really exclusive, something that nobody else has done before!'

The party organizer had a brilliant idea: he decided to arrange a safari Bar Mitzvah deep in the African jungle. The expedition was organized, more than 200 guests were invited, and a special plane was chartered. At the small landing strip in the jungle the guests were met by a unique attraction – a caravan of 200 elephants! Each elephant wore a sash bearing the name of the Bar Mitzvah boy. The guests were helped on to their elephants, and they awaited the signal to set off to the place where the great Bar Mitzvah banquet was to be held.

'What are we waiting for?' asked the father. The highly embarrassed party organizer answered, 'They're just clearing the tables after the last Bar Mitzvah!'

✡

M oishe and Yossi were having a discussion about the Vietnam War, which was overshadowing all American youth. Moishe was very pessimistic about his future, and he was very worried about whether he would ever be able to finish his studies. Yossi, on the other hand, was most optimistic.

'You'll manage your exams,' Yossi assured Moishe. 'You don't have to worry about it. This war will soon be over, and even if it's not, there are always two possibilities: either you are called up or you're not. If you're not called up, you don't have reason to worry, but even if you are, there are still two possibilities: either they send you to Vietnam or they don't. If you're not sent, you needn't worry, and if you are sent, there are still two possibilities: either you get wounded or you don't. If you don't, there's no reason to worry, but even if you do, there are still two possibilities: either the wound is serious or it isn't. If it isn't, you've no reason to worry, but even if it is, there still remain two possibilities: either you survive or you don't. If you survive, you've no reason to worry. The only reason to worry is if you don't survive. Now I ask you, is it worth worrying about such a remote possibility?'

✡

Three Jewish ladies in Brooklyn were, as one would expect, having a chat about their sons. One lady said, 'My Harry, he's such a successful doctor that he earns at least $200,000 per year!'

The second lady said, 'And my Stephen, he's such a successful lawyer that he earns at least $150,000 per year!'

'And how much does your son earn?' the first two asked the third mother.

'He's a rabbi,' she replied. 'His annual salary is $40,000.'

'What – a rabbi?!' the first two ladies exclaimed in disbelief. 'Is that a job for a Jewish boy?'

✡

An American businessman, who happened to be a Catholic, and his Jewish business partner each bought the same type of Cadillac on the same day. The Catholic asked his parish priest to bless his new car. The priest took some holy water and sprinkled it on the Cadillac. The Jewish businessman, not wishing to be outdone, asked his rabbi to bless his car as well. At first the rabbi was a little non-plussed, but then he decided exactly what to do, and cut off a small piece of the exhaust pipe!

✡

On his way home one Friday evening Rosenbaum passed by his synagogue and saw a poster announcing, 'Tomorrow the rabbi will preach on the theme of "The Great Flood and its devastating consequences".'

At home, Rosenbaum sat down and wrote a short letter to the rabbi: 'Dear Rabbi, I'm sorry to say that I can't come tomorrow morning. However, I do wish to fulfil my responsibilities. Please find enclosed a $100 cheque for the victims of the flood.'

✡

On the day of Yom Kippur, Bloomfield, a successful broker on Wall Street, said to his young, non-Jewish assistant, 'Jimmy, today is the holiest day for us Jews, and I have to go to synagogue on Fifth Avenue. I don't want to be disturbed while I'm there, unless something extraordinary happens in the market.'

Hardly half an hour after Bloomfield had gone the market was in real trouble. The price of gold had dropped a full ten points. Jimmy didn't know whether to buy or to sell, yet he didn't wish to disturb his boss at his prayers. He decided to wait.

When the gold price dropped a further five points, Jimmy had no choice but to ask his boss for advice. He went to the synagogue and found his boss near to the front in the middle of a long row of praying Jews. With some difficulty, Jimmy made his way along the row and whispered to his boss, 'Something terrible has happened, sir! The gold price has dropped fifteen points!'

Bloomfield whispered his reply: 'Now look, you've burdened yourself with a threefold guilt. First, because you disturbed my prayers on Yom Kippur; second, because you disturbed all the people who had to get up to let you pass; and third, because you're not up to date. You talk of a fifteen-point drop, when the gold price in the synagogue is already trading at twenty points lower!'

✡

For the High Holy Days the great Temple Emmanuel Synagogue on Fifth Avenue, New York, had booked the famous Cantor Kussevitsky. Accordingly, an entrance fee was requested from each member of the congregation. A young man came and asked for admission, but when asked for his ticket he explained that he only wanted to say something important to his uncle, who was already in the synagogue. The Shammes,[2] full of suspicion, said, 'OK, you can come in, but I warn you – I'd better not catch you praying!'

✡

In a small town in Virginia a man applied for the job of Cantor. He was invited to demonstrate his talent during the Friday evening service. When he returned home, his wife asked him how things had gone at the synagogue.

'Bad,' he replied. 'The Shammes told me that my efforts were awful.'

'Aah, why do you listen to the opinion of the Shammes?' his wife said comfortingly. 'Everybody knows that the Shammes only ever repeats what others are saying!'

✡

A Chinese man sat in the cafeteria of a New York airport drinking a cup of tea. Shlomo Goldberg walked in, saw the man, introduced himself, struck the man across the face and said, 'That was for Pearl Harbor!'

'But that was the Japanese!' replied the astonished Chinese man.

'Japanese, Chinese – they're all the same to me!' answered Goldberg.

Now the Chinese man slapped Goldberg in the face. 'That's for the *Titanic*!' he said.

'But that was the fault of an iceberg!'

'Iceberg, Goldberg — they're all the same to me!'

As he was strolling through Brooklyn, Yossi passed an ice-cream parlour which was displaying a sign saying 'Jews Not Wanted'. He rushed in to protest to the anti-Semitic owner, and whom did he find? Moishe Bernstein!

'What's the matter with you?' asked Yossi. 'Why isn't a Jew allowed into your cafe?'

'Have you tried my ice cream?' whispered Moishe.

✡

Ten-year-old Mottel, a bright Jewish boy, wanted to take part in a Catholic religious education class. He took a place in the back row and listened. The priest said, 'Children, today I'm going to ask you a question, and whoever gives the right answer will get five dollars. My question is: Who was the most important man in world history?'

One boy said, 'Napoleon.'

'No,' replied the priest, 'he was a great man, but not the greatest.'

A second boy said, 'Julius Caesar.'

'No.'

A third boy: 'George Washington.'

'Again, no.'

At that moment Mottel stood up and said, 'Jesus Christ!'

'That's the right answer!' said the priest. 'And you'll get the five dollars. But you're a Jewish boy – why didn't you say Moses?'

'I'll tell you, Father,' answered Mottel. 'Moses is Moses but business is business!'

✡

Two New York Jews were walking through an area of dubious reputation when two huge men approached them menacingly.

'Let's get out of here quickly!' said one Jew to the other. 'There are two of them, and we're alone!'

✡

An assimilated American Jew was in utter despair because his wife had been in the maternity ward for two days with no sign of giving birth. He consulted his rabbi, who advised him to invite ten religious Jews into his house to recite psalms so that the Almighty would show mercy to the poor woman and hasten the birth.

The man followed the rabbi's advice and, lo and behold, the ten Jews had hardly been praying for one hour when the maternity nurse happily told the man that his wife had given birth to a girl. Two minutes later the nurse returned and said, 'It's not one girl – it's two!'

The young man ran to the phone and told the people at home, 'Stop praying!'

On Broadway the minister of the local Scottish church noticed that a shop had a huge sign at the front saying, 'Goldberg and Macintosh'. He entered the shop and was welcomed by a bearded man wearing a kippa.

'I'm glad to see one of your people and one of my people as business partners,' said the minister. 'That's a pleasant surprise!'

'I've got an even bigger surprise for you,' said the bearded man, ''cos I'm Macintosh!'

✡

An elderly Jewish lady boarded an El Al plane in New York to fly to Tel Aviv. In her arms she was holding a small basket, inside which was a little dog.

'I would like to keep this basket on my lap during the flight,' the woman said to the steward.

'I'm sorry, madam, but that isn't allowed.'

'I want to keep my dog with me!' cried the woman.

The steward reassured her that the dog would have its own place in the cargo hold and that she needn't worry. The lady gave in and handed the basket to the steward.

Upon their arrival at Ben Gurion Airport, the steward took the basket out of the cargo hold and discovered with horror that the dog was dead! What could he tell the lady? He asked a colleague for help.

'Look, this is a light brown Cocker Spaniel,' said the colleague. 'I'll drive to Tel Aviv and find a similar one – the lady won't know the difference.'

While his colleague went to Tel Aviv, the steward told the lady that the dog had to be quarantined for a few hours. Eventually his colleague returned with a new dog, and the steward handed dog and basket back to the lady.

'Here is your dog, Madam.'

The lady glanced at the dog and cried, 'That's not my dog!'

'But it *is* your dog, Madam!'

'It is *not* my dog!'

'Why are you so sure that it's not your dog?'

'Because my dog is dead. I wanted to bury him in the Holy Land!'

✡

Moishe and Hymie had each opened a barber's shop in the same street, and now they were competing for customers. Moishe put up a huge sign in his window: 'Haircut — only $8!'

The following day Hymie put up a sign in his window: 'Haircut — only $6!'

The following morning Moishe added another sign to the first: 'For $2 we put right the haircuts done by the establishment along the road.'

✡

In a busy street in Manhattan an Irish-born American opened a new restaurant. A sign in the window said, 'The best restaurant in the whole of Manhattan'. A few days later a second Irish-born American opened a restaurant just two doors away. A sign in his window claimed, 'The best restaurant in this street'. An American Jew then rented the empty shop between the two restaurants. He converted it into a restaurant and put up his sign: 'Entrance here'.

✡

The managing board of the New Reform Synagogue in Brooklyn sent the following letter to its members:

In order to guarantee you a place next to members sharing your interests, we ask you to tick the appropriate boxes below:

DURING THE SERVICE I PREFER SITTING NEXT TO MEMBERS WHO:

Talk about the stockmarkets ☐
Comment on the sports news ☐
Prefer social gossip ☐
Sit still and pray ☐

✡

A huge Buick limousine stopped at the door of the synagogue. A big man smoking a big cigar got out and asked for the rabbi. The two men went into the rabbi's office and he locked the door from the inside. The shammes listened at the keyhole and caught the following pieces of conversation:

'I'll give $100,000 to your synagogue,' said the visitor.

'No,' replied the rabbi.

'$200,000, then!'

'No!'

'How about $500,000?!'

'No way!'

After the disappointed visitor had left the shammes asked the rabbi why he had refused such a generous donation, since the money would have been very useful.

'Do you know what he wanted in exchange?!' cried the irate rabbi. 'All our prayers on the High Holy Days would have to end not with "Amen" but with "Coca Cola"!'

In a circus in New York Hercules the strong man was impressing the audiences with his muscle power. He lifted objects weighing hundreds of pounds, he punched holes in brick walls and, for his finale, with one hand he squeezed a lemon so hard that not one drop of juice was left in the fruit.

The Ringmaster entered the arena and, in a challenging tone, said, 'I will pay $200 to anyone who is capable of squeezing just one drop from this lemon!'

Two strong men came forward. Each of them tried vainly to squeeze one drop from the lemon.

'Is there anyone else who wants to have a try?' asked the Ringmaster.

A little Jewish man stepped forward, and the audience sneered. The man took the lemon, squeezed it and, behold – a miracle! – not only a drop but lots of juice flowed from the lemon!

The astonished Ringmaster gave the man the promised $200 and asked, 'Would you mind telling me who you are and what your profession is?'

'I'm a collector for the United Jewish Appeal Fund,' answered the little man.

A collector for a well-known Jewish charity visited the wealthy Max Bernstein to ask him for a donation. The industrialist, who was famed for his meanness, said, 'I'm ready to make a large donation, upon the condition that it remains anonymous.'

'I guarantee that no one will ever hear about it,' said the collector.

Bernstein took out his cheque-book and wrote a cheque for over $500. The collector thanked him but then realized that the cheque had not been signed.

'You've forgotten to sign it, sir,' he said.

Bernstein replied, 'I told you, didn't I, that the donation must remain anonymous!'

✡

A group of American Jewish tourists on safari were captured by a tribe of cannibals. The prisoners were tied up and the tribal chief was summoned to decide which recipe to use in cooking them. The chief saw that one of the prisoners was wearing a Star of David upon a chain around his neck.

'What?!' he exclaimed in perfect Yiddish. 'Are you a Jew?'

'We're all Jews!' answered the man. 'And you? How come you speak such perfect Yiddish?'

'Ah, that's a long story,' said the chief. 'One day a tourist got lost in the jungle, and we took him back to our village. He told us beautiful stories from the Bible and gradually converted us to Judaism and taught us Yiddish and the Jewish traditions.'

The chief freed the prisoners at once. 'They share our faith,' he told his people.

That evening there was a party in honour of the guests. A young tribesman, dressed in animal skins and feathers and swinging a spear, performed some exotic dances. His mother, wearing her ceremonial dress, turned to the man with the Star of David and proudly said, 'Do you see him? He's my son, the doctor!'

✡

At the annual meeting of the American Conference of Rabbis, the chairperson announced the following agenda item: 'Now follows discussion about the problems which rabbis have with the managing boards of their synagogues. All rabbis who have no problems with their managing boards will meet in half an hour on the second floor in the telephone box.'

---

[1] The Yiddish word *Goy* means 'non-Jew'.

[2] The caretaker of a synagogue.

14
ISRAEL

The bureaucracy of the Israeli government is an endless source of jokes. In many countries jokes are made about civil servants, but those told in Israel are particularly biting.

With great effort a snail was creeping along the motorway between Tel Aviv and Jerusalem. Feeling sorry for the snail, a passing driver stopped and said to it, 'Let me save you all this effort! I'll tell you what – I'll put you in an envelope and send you by post to Jerusalem.'

'That's very kind of you,' said the snail, 'but I'm really in a hurry!'

Until recently, every Israeli who wanted to travel abroad had to pay an export tax of £150. One day, an Israeli wished to travel with his wife and four children to Spain, and had to pay £900. He was understandably angry with the Finance Ministry, especially as he had to queue for hours to pay his tax. After half an hour he left the queue and said out loud, 'I'm now going to the Finance Ministry to kill the Minister!'

One hour later he returned. The queue at the tax office was still just as long. Some curious people asked him if he had succeeded in killing the Finance Minister. 'Ah, no,' he answered. 'The queue there was even longer than the one here!'

✡

The Director of an Israeli Government office was inspecting his various departments. It was January, and in one of the offices a civil servant was sitting with the window wide open.

'Aren't you afraid of catching a cold?' asked the Director.

'Oh no, absolutely not,' replied the civil servant. 'I'm used to sleeping with the window wide open!'

✡

For ten years Yossi had eaten daily in the same restaurant in Tel Aviv. Each lunchtime he started with potato soup. One day, after he had been served with his soup, he said to the waiter, 'I want you to try this soup.'

'Why? It's the same soup that I give you every day.'

'But I still want you to try the soup!'

'If you don't like this bowl of soup, I'll bring you another one.'

'I don't want another one. I just want you to try this soup.'

'All right, if I must. Where's the spoon?'

'Aha!'

✡

The first Zionist pioneers who emigrated to Palestine in the 1920s and who created the foundations of today's Israel came mainly from Czarist Russia. They brought several Russian habits with them, one of which was tea-drinking. This habit is retained to this day with almost religious fervour in all government offices, as the following anecdote shows.

Two lions had escaped from the Tel Aviv Zoo, and it took more than two weeks of intensive hunting to recapture them. One of the two was terribly emaciated, while the other was well fed. This lion asked the other how he came to be so thin. The thin lion replied that he had escaped into the Negev Desert, where there was no food at all.

'And how come you look so well fed?' asked the thin lion.

'I had a really bright idea. I stayed around the government offices. Each day I ate a civil servant, and no one noticed!'

'Is that so? How did they manage to catch you, then?'

'Oh, one day I made a big mistake – I ate the tea-lady!'

✡

A civil servant in the Israeli Ministry of Agriculture visited an Arab farmer in Galilee to help him with the rationalization of his farm.

'How much milk do your cows give, Mohammed?' asked the civil servant.

'Eight to ten litres per day,' answered the farmer.

'That's not good enough. You must get yourself Dutch cows. They give at least fifteen to twenty litres per day.'

'Impossible!' said Mohammed.

'Well, I'll prove it to you. I'll bring you a Dutch cow from one of our *kibbutzim*. I'll leave it with you for two weeks, and you'll see for yourself that I'm right.'

The civil servant went off and brought back a cow named Aviva and left her with Mohammed. After two weeks he returned and asked, 'Well, who was right, then?'

'I was right,' said Mohammed. 'Your cow doesn't give any more milk than mine – eight to ten litres per day.'

'Impossible!' declared the civil servant. He ran into the barn and shouted at Aviva, 'What's the matter with you? In the *kibbutz* you used to give twenty litres of milk daily!'

'How can you compare the two?' replied Aviva. 'In the *kibbutz* I was a member of the commune, but here I'm a government servant!'

✡

*A*n *Israeli riddle:* What's this: four in a room, three don't work, one does? The answer: three civil servants and one electric fan!

✡

*I*n 1949, just after the War of Independence, the young state of Israel had to cope with a mass immigration of Jews from the Arab countries, and so found itself in great financial difficulty. The Finance Minister, Caplan, briefed Prime Minister David Ben-Gurion about the situation.

Ben-Gurion said to Caplan, 'You've got such a clever brain – do you have some ideas about how to get us out of this mess?'

'Yes, I have a brilliant idea,' answered Caplan. 'We should do the same as the Germans did, and declare war on America. America will defeat us and will then support our economy!'

'That really is a great idea!' said Ben-Gurion. 'But what do we do if we defeat America? How do we find the money to support 200 million Americans?'

✡

1965. Finance Minister Levi Eshkol was complaining to Prime Minister David Ben-Gurion about the bad economic state of the nation. Ben-Gurion said, 'Do you have any idea how we can get out of this mess?'

'I have a proposal,' replied Eshkol, 'but I'm not sure you'll like it.'

'Well, what is it?'

'Who says we have to be a republic? We could turn Israel into a monarchy. We could install a king with a royal court. Just imagine it – a Jewish king, after a lapse of 2,000 years! Tourists would come from all over the world to admire a Jewish king! The economy would recover and the country would be saved.'

'That's not a bad idea!' said Ben-Gurion. 'But who's going to be king?'

'You, of course!'

'What, I should become David the Second? Never!'

✡

Finance Minister Levi Eshkol had travelled to Washington to discuss the possibility of an American loan. He asked the American Finance Minister how much the average American earned.

'About $2,000 per month,' was the answer.

'How much does he need to lead a decent life?'

'About $1,200.'

'What does he do with the balance each month?'

The American Finance Minister, somewhat piqued, replied, 'We're not interested in what he does with it – after all, we're a democracy! But while we're talking about it, how much does the average Israeli earn?'

'About £1,000.'

'And how much does he need to live?'

'About £2,000.'

'Where does he get the extra £1,000 from?'

Now Eshkol, also somewhat piqued, said, 'We're not interested in where he gets it from – after all, we're a democracy!'

Anew-born baby had been abandoned by its mother at the entrance to an Israeli government building. The policeman who was called to deal with the matter said to the Director of the department, 'I assume that one of your civil servants is the father of this baby – otherwise the mother wouldn't have abandoned the child here.'

'With my hand on my heart I can promise you that it wasn't one of my staff,' replied the Director. 'Not one of my civil servants has ever created anything with love and enthusiasm!'

1946. Jerusalem was besieged by the Arab Legion, and food and water were running low. The mood among the people was very subdued, except for Moishe the greengrocer, who always had a cheery word to lift people's spirits. 'Don't worry,' he would say. 'All will be well! We'll be saved!'

'We're starving,' the people replied, 'and who's going to save us?'

'Either we'll be saved in a natural way or by a miracle.'

'Which is the natural way?' the people asked.

'The natural way is that God will come to our aid, as he has always done.'

'And what's the miracle?'

'The miracle will be when our troops break through the enemy lines!'

✡

1960. A KGB agent had been sent to Israel to spy. His orders were to contact an Israeli Communist named Rabinowitz who lived in Tel Aviv at 123 Ben-Gurion Street. The recognition code was 'In Korea the sun shines.'

The spy found the house, but discovered that within this one building there were four families named Rabinowitz. He tried his luck with the first Rabinowitz, who lived on the ground floor. He rang the bell, and a man appeared at the door.

'Can I help you?' he asked.

'In Korea the sun shines,' said the KGB man.

'Oh, you're looking for Rabinowitz the spy! Third floor, on the right.'

✡

For 30 years the Israeli Labour Party was the dominant party in government, occupying the most important ministerial posts. Although it always had to make coalitions with smaller parties because it never had an absolute majority, it practically ruled the whole political scene in the new state. Many people were upset by its high-handedness, as the following anecdote illustrates.

*T*el Aviv. An Israeli employee in the American Embassy was astonished to see a man whom he knew to be a fervent Zionist standing in the queue for emigration to the USA.

'Hyam, what are you doing here?'

'I want to emigrate to America.'

'You can't be serious! You, a veteran Zionist, want to leave Israel? What happened?'

'Well, let me tell you. The people are unhappy with the ruling Labour Party. It won't be long before an opposition party from the left or the right comes to power. Whichever way it goes, for us long-term Labour Party comrades it will be the end of our power. So I've decided to leave before events overtake me.'

'But Hyam, you've really got it wrong! Labour has a firm grip on power, and it will govern for decades to come in Israel!'

'Now, that's exactly the reason why I'm leaving!'

✡

Rolf Pauls, West Germany's first Ambassador to Israel, handed over his letters of appointment to the Israeli President and expressed the wish to lay a wreath at the grave of the Unknown Soldier.

The Israeli Chief of Protocol was non-plussed by this request: there was no such grave in Israel! He quickly recovered and said to the Ambassador, 'Come with me, sir. I'll take you there.'

He drove to the Tel Aviv cemetery and led the Ambassador to the very impressive grave of a famous industrialist. 'Here is the grave, your Excellency.'

The Ambassador laid the wreath, bowed respectfully and asked his companion to translate the Hebrew inscription.

The Chief of Protocol had no choice but to translate exactly: 'Here rests the industrialist so and so...'

'But you told me that this was the grave of the Unknown Soldier!'

'Oh, but it is! As an industrialist he was very well known, but as a soldier he was completely unknown!'

✡

Willy Brandt once visited Shlomo Lahat, the Lord Mayor of Tel Aviv, who took him on a sight-seeing tour. One of the famous sights was the concert hall which had been donated by an American Jewish millionaire.

'I'm glad to see,' said Brandt, 'that this hall is dedicated to the great German writer Thomas Mann.'

'I must disappoint you, Herr Brandt,' answered Lahat, 'but it's named after Frederick Mann, not Thomas Mann.'

'Oh, and what did Frederick Mann write?'

'A huge cheque!'

✡

The Mayor of an Israeli town was walking with his wife past a building site. The builder saw the two and greeted the woman by her first name. The Mayor, slightly surprised, said, 'This man seems to know you well. Who is he?'

'We were at school together,' his wife answered, 'and he even proposed to me.'

'Aren't you lucky, my love, to have married me and not him – otherwise you would now be the wife of a builder and not the wife of a Mayor!'

'No, I'm afraid you're wrong, dear. If I had married him, *he* would be the Mayor today!'

✡

Dr Moishe Sneh was one of the most prominent figures in the Haganah, the defence organization which had been formed by the Jewish settlers in Palestine before the creation of the state of Israel. He later became a member of the tiny Israeli Communist Party and was its representative in the Knesset.

One day, when an important political debate came to an end and all the deputies were gathered in the main chamber for the final vote, one deputy saw Dr Sneh outside having a glass of orange juice, as if he had all the time in the world.

'What are you doing out here?' asked the deputy. 'The vote is going to take place at any moment!'

'Unlike you, I don't need to worry,' replied Dr Sneh. 'Nobody threatens my minority!'

✡

Moshe Shapira was the President of the National Religious Party and the head of the Ministries of the Interior, Health and Culture. A long-serving party member once asked him for a job in one of his three Ministries.

'You're lucky,' said Shapira. 'The post of Director of the Department of Communal Administration in the Ministry of the Interior is vacant. You can have it!'

'But I haven't the faintest idea about Communal Administration!' said the party member. 'Haven't you got anything else?'

'Yes, I could give you the post of Director of the Department of Epidemiology in the Health Ministry.'

'What do I know about Epidemiology? Haven't you got anything else?'

'If you like I can offer you the post of Director of Extraterrestrial Signs in the Desert in the Ministry of Culture.'

'Now you're joking at my expense, aren't you? What do I know about extraterrestrials? Couldn't you just give me a simple post in one of your Ministries?'

'I'm sorry, but to be a simple employee requires expert knowledge!'

✡

As the American army in Vietnam was fighting the Viet Cong with no prospect of a final victory, Richard Nixon turned to the Israeli Government. He asked if they could send the legendary General Moshe Dayan, who had recently defeated the Egyptian army, to advise the American generals on a successful strategy in Vietnam.

'We're willing to do so,' was the Israeli answer. 'We'll lend you General Dayan, but in exchange we want two American generals!'

'No problem!' said Nixon. 'Name the two.'

'General Motors and General Electric!'

✡

In contrast to Menachim Begin who, as Opposition Leader, came daily to the Knesset, David Ben-Gurion only turned up when there was an important vote on the agenda. Consequently a Ben-Gurion autograph was a highly prized rarity.

One day a student came to Begin and asked him for his autograph, which Begin happily gave. Ten minutes later the same student asked Begin for a second autograph. Again he obliged. When the student asked for a third autograph, however, Begin lost his temper.

'Two of my autographs aren't enough, eh?!' he snapped.

'What can I do, s-s-sir,' stammered the student, 'when for ten Begins I can hardly get one Ben-Gurion!'

✡

David Ben-Gurion's Jerusalem home was in Rehaviah, a part of the city mainly inhabited by German Jews. One morning he greeted a neighbour in Hebrew. The neighbour replied, 'I'm so sorry, Prime Minister, but I don't speak Hebrew.'

'How long now have you been living in Israel?' asked Ben-Gurion.

'Thirty years, Prime Minister!'

'Thirty years, and you're not ashamed that you can't speak Hebrew?'

'You know, it's so much easier to be ashamed than to learn Hebrew!'

✡

Many jokes have been told about Pola Ben-Gurion, the wife of the great Israeli Prime Minister. Here are two of them:

Zippora Sharett, the cultured wife of the Israeli Foreign Minister, asked Pola Ben-Gurion whether she had enjoyed seeing *The Marriage of Figaro*. Pola replied, 'I can't attend every wedding – I send them flowers!'

✡

Ben-Gurion and his wife had been invited to the opening concert of the winter season of the Israeli Philharmonic Orchestra. They arrived late and the concert had already started.

Pola asked her neighbour what was being played at that moment. The neighbour whispered that it was Beethoven's *Ninth Symphony*.

Pola said to her husband, 'David, let's go home – we've already missed eight symphonies!'

✡

An old friend of Prime Minister Ben-Gurion was complaining to him that he had been overlooked in the recent Cabinet reshuffle.

'You're right,' said Ben-Gurion, 'but now, sadly, it's too late. There are no posts left.'

The friend said, 'Couldn't you create a new Ministry? For example, a Ministry for the Colonies?'

'But we haven't got any colonies!'

'In that case, why do we have a Ministry of Finance?!'

✡

'Everyone can make a small fortune in Israel.'
'How?'
'By coming to Israel with a large one!'

✡

It is common knowledge that David Ben-Gurion couldn't stand Menachem Begin, the long-time leader of the opposition Likud Party. The day after Ben-Gurion's dramatic exit from government and total retirement from political life, the telephone rang at his home. Pola, his wife, answered and said, 'Who is speaking?'

'It's Menachem Begin here. May I please speak to the Prime Minister?'

'But Mr Begin, you know that my husband is no longer the Prime Minister.'

Ten minutes later the phone rang again. 'Menachem Begin here. May I now please speak to the Prime Minister?'

'But Mr Begin, I've already told you that my husband is no longer the Prime Minister! Why are you calling again?'

'Because it's so satisfying to hear that your husband is no longer the Prime Minister!'

✡

Ben-Gurion had died. In Heaven above they were considering how to treat him. As the founder of the state of Israel, he deserved Paradise, but on the other hand, as a non-believer he would probably find the company there too pious. They decided to let him choose between Paradise and Hell.

He decided to have a look at both. Paradise was quite beautiful but, indeed, he didn't feel too happy among so many rabbis. When he saw Hell, he was surprised at how pleasant it seemed. People were sitting comfortably around a table, chatting amiably, and even the food was quite good.

'I'll go to Hell!' decided Ben-Gurion.

He had hardly spoken when the whole scene changed, and he was led into a real Hell with fire and brimstone.

'But you showed me something quite different before!' complained Ben-Gurion to the angel who had guided him.

'That's right,' said the angel, 'but then you were a tourist – now you're a new immigrant!'

✡

A pious Catholic had travelled to Israel to visit all the Christian holy places. He arrived at Lake Tiberias, where he was offered a boat trip to the far side.

'How much is the fare?' he asked the boatman.

'Fifty shekels.'

'So much money for such a short trip!'

'You mustn't forget, sir, that this is no ordinary lake. It's the lake on which Jesus walked!'

'With such a high boat fare, I'm not surprised that he did walk!'

An American Jewish tourist wanted to go to the West Wall of Jerusalem, and he asked his Israeli taxi driver to take him to the 'Wailing Wall'.

The driver replied, 'Sorry, I don't know what you mean.'

The tourist said in Yiddish, '*Brengt mich dorten, wu die Jden wajnen!*' ('Take me to where the Jews are crying!')

'Oh, I see!' said the driver, and promptly took him to the tax office.

✡

Dr Aron Barth was the first Director General of the Israeli National Bank. Being an Orthodox Jew, he wore his kippa all day in the office. When asked by the American Finance Minister whether it was really necessary for him to always wear his kippa, he replied, 'Of course it is! This is the only cover there is for the Israeli Lira!'

✡

During the Korean War the political parties in Israel were divided. The left-wing Mapam Party felt a need to send a brigade of volunteers to North Korea to fight alongside the Communist army. The right-wing Cherut Party decided to send a brigade of volunteers to South Korea to support the fight against the Communists.

When both parties urged the acting Finance Minister, Pinchas Sapir, to give them the funds to buy travel tickets for their volunteers, the Minister had a brilliant idea.

'Why should we use our small foreign currency reserves to send these two groups to Korea, where they will fight each other?' he asked. 'I propose that the two brigades do their fighting here in Israel!'

✡

In the 1970s the Israeli currency was hit by a double-figure monthly rate of inflation, which gave rise to many anecdotes. Here are two of them:

Why is it cheaper in today's Israel to travel by taxi rather than by bus? Because with a bus you pay before the journey, but with a taxi you pay afterwards!

✡

An American astronaut landed on Mars and, to his great astonishment, found an Israeli who was just about to raise the Israeli flag.

'How did you manage to get up here?' asked the American.

'Pretty simple, really. I climbed with the prices in Israel!'

'And how do you plan to get down again?'

'With the Israeli Lira!'

✡

An American Jew and an Israeli met in Paris in the Cafe de la Paix. The American asked, 'Do you know the United States?'

'I've never been there,' answered the Israeli.

'Have you ever heard of the Empire State Building?'

'Of course!'

The American said proudly, 'My father built that! And have you heard of the Brooklyn Bridge? My father built that too. And who do you think built the White House in Washington? My father!'

This was too much for the Israeli, who said, 'And you, I'm sure, have heard of the Dead Sea?'

'But of course! What about it?'

'Well, let me tell you – my father killed it!'

✡

In a Tel Aviv restaurant an American tourist said to the waiter, 'Hey man, switch on the air conditioning! I can hardly breathe in here!'

The waiter politely said, 'Very well, sir.'

A few minutes later the customer called him again: 'Hey waiter, switch off the air conditioning! I'm freezing to death!'

The waiter calmly said, 'Very well, sir.'

Within five minutes the American was again asking for the air conditioning to be switched on: 'I can't breathe!'

Another tourist who had witnessed the whole incident said to the waiter, 'I admire your patience – switching on, switching off! The man doesn't know what he wants!'

The waiter bent down to the tourist and whispered, 'Let him grumble! To tell you the truth — we don't have an air conditioner!'

✡

An American Jew who had emigrated to Israel ordered a telephone on the day of his arrival. Having heard nothing for three weeks, he went to the Post Office to enquire about his application.

'When did you make your application?' asked the clerk.

The American gave him the exact date.

'But that's only a few weeks ago! There are many other people who applied before you.'

'Does that mean,' said the American, 'that there isn't any hope for me?'

'Oh no!' the clerk replied. 'A Jew may never say that there is no hope. However, he may say that there isn't the slightest chance!'

✡

An American tourist was about to leave Israel after a stay of two weeks. His Israeli cousin took him to Ben-Gurion Airport and asked him, 'Be honest – what do you think about our little country?'

The tourist answered, 'It's very beautiful. There's only one thing I have a problem with – you Israelis are constantly talking about food, work and housing. We in America, on the other hand, talk about art, literature and culture.'

The Israeli thoughtfully said, 'Yes, you may have a point. Everybody probably talks about those things they miss the most!'

✡

A rich Jewish farmer from Texas was visiting his cousin in an Israeli *kibbutz*. The Israeli showed him the hen-house, the cows, the dining-room and so on. The Texan, whose farm was a hundred times larger than the *kibbutz*, smiled kindly and said, 'You know, I've got a farm too. When I take my car out in the morning to inspect my land, I still haven't finished my tour by the evening.'

His cousin, full of understanding, said, 'Oh, I know exactly what you mean! We used to have an unreliable car too!'

✡

A bove the entrance to a Tel Aviv restaurant a big sign said: 'All European Languages Spoken'. A tourist entered and spoke to the owner in English. The owner tried to explain with his hands that he didn't understand a word.

The tourist then tried French, German, Spanish and Russian, all without any success. Finally he found a passer-by who spoke English. He asked him to ask the owner in Hebrew who the person was who spoke 'all European languages', as it said on the sign. The owner replied, 'The customers!'

✡

A fter the Six-Day War Israel had to accommodate hundreds of thousands of Egyptian prisoners of war. Moshe Dayan, on being asked if the Israelis might take bitter revenge on the Egyptian prisoners, said with a smile, 'The only revenge that our soldiers are going to take is that they are going to feed the prisoners with the same grub as they have in their own canteen!'

✡

An American tourist was standing in Dizengoff Street in Tel Aviv and staring at something. Several passers-by gathered round him and began to stare as well. Within fifteen minutes a small crowd had formed, and they were all staring. A policeman saw this gathering and asked what it was all about.

'We don't know,' said one of the crowd. 'Ask the tourist!'

He did so, and the tourist said, 'I'm admiring those two statues on the other side of the road.'

'But there are no statues in Dizengoff Street!'

'Yes there are! Look for yourself!'

'Do you mean those two over there? They're workmen!'

'Strange,' said the tourist. 'I've been standing here for more than half an hour, and they haven't moved once!'

✡

An American Jew from Texas who was used to travelling thousands of miles in his car visited Israel. At Tel Aviv Airport he was picked up by a taxi which had been arranged for him by his travel agent. It was eight o'clock in the morning.

'Where are we going?' the Texan asked his driver.

'I suggest we make a circular tour of all Israel.'

To which the Texan replied, 'And what are we going to do in the afternoon?'

✡

Five young recruits to the Israeli Army were allowed one day's leave in order to celebrate the Sabbath at home. The one condition was that they had to return to their unit by 6.00 a.m. on the Sunday.

They all returned on Sunday, but two hours late. The Sergeant was furious and shouted at the first recruit, 'What excuse do you have for being back at this time?'

'I have to report that I live in a *kibbutz* and can ride a horse, so I thought that rather than wait for the bus, I would take a horse and ride back to the barracks. But what do you think happened? The horse collapsed and died, and I had to wait two hours for the bus!'

The Sergeant didn't believe a word of this, but he accepted the excuse. He then asked the second recruit, 'And what's your excuse?'

'I'm also from a *kibbutz* and I also took a horse which collapsed and died, and I too had to wait two hours for the bus!'

The third and fourth recruits told the same story. The Sergeant, by now at the end of his tether, shouted at the fifth recruit, 'I'm warning you – you'd better not tell me that you rode a horse that collapsed!'

'Nothing of the sort, Sergeant! I took the bus, but it couldn't get through because the road was covered with dead horses!'

✡

A colonel in the Israeli Air Force had the task of buying a new jet fighter which would cost at least $50 million. To pay for the plane he intended to contact 1,000 rich American Jews, each of whom would donate $50,000. He told a colleague about his brilliant idea.

'But the plane will never even take off,' said the colleague.

'Why?'

'Do you have any idea how much 1,000 donation plaques weigh?'

✡

A twenty-year-old man who had emigrated from the Soviet Union to Israel was called up to do his military service. In the recruiting office he was being asked which of the three forces he wished to join: the Navy, the Army or the Air Force.

'If I can choose, then the Navy, please.'

The recruiting officer took a form and began to ask the man his surname, first name, date of birth, place of birth, educational level and so forth. To the question, 'Can you swim?' the man reacted sharply, 'Why – don't you have any ships?!'

✡

B en-Gurion Airport. A group of recently arrived immigrants from the Soviet Union were being questioned by some journalists.

'How is the economic situation in today's Russia?'

'One can't complain.'

'How about housing?'

'One can't complain.'

'How about anti-Semitism?'

'One can't complain.'

'If that's the case, why have you emigrated to Israel?'

'Because here one *can* complain!'

✡

Three men were seated together in a train: a Russian, a Scotsman and an Israeli. The Russian took a tin of caviare from his luggage, nibbled a small amount of it and then threw the nearly full tin out of the window. His two companions stared at him in disbelief. The Russian said, 'You see, in Russia we have so much caviare!'

Now the Scotsman took out a bottle of whisky, drank a mouthful of it and threw the nearly full bottle out of the window. The others stared at him in disbelief. 'Well, you see,' said the Scotsman, 'in Scotland we have so much whisky!'

The Israeli, not wishing to be outdone, grabbed the Russian by the collar and threw him through the window. The Scotsman looked at him in horror. The Israeli calmly said, 'Well, you see, in Israel we have so many Russians!'

✡

An angel was ordered to descend and report on the situation on earth. He returned in a state of utter confusion. When asked what had confused him so much, he replied, 'The world is completely upside down! The Jews are now the best soldiers and the Germans are doing the best business!'

✡

Three men were sitting in a cafe in Tel Aviv: an architect, a surgeon and a politician. They were discussing which of their three professions was the oldest.

The surgeon said, 'It's obvious that my profession came first. God sent Adam to sleep and took a rib out of his rib-cage. A surgical procedure with anaesthetic!'

The architect said, 'Maybe, but before God created Adam he formed the world out of chaos. A real achievement in architecture!'

The politician said triumphantly, 'Yes, but who created the chaos?!'

✡

The Israeli Minister of Finance had travelled to the United States to request a desperately needed loan of $500 million. When walking through Brooklyn, he saw a Jewish beggar who was asking for some change. He gave a dollar to the man, who said to him, 'I think I know your face – aren't you the Israeli Finance Minister?' 'When the Minister nodded in agreement, the beggar said to him, 'Here, take your dollar back – I won't take money from a colleague!'

✡

Shimon Peres, when he was the Israeli Foreign Minister, visited the American President, Bill Clinton. He asked Clinton, 'Mr President, are all United States citizens happy with your policies?'

'Well,' replied Clinton, 'I don't think that one can expect 200 million people to be happy with every policy. I'm sure that there are three to four million who aren't pleased with me. But how is it with you in Israel, Mr Peres?'

Peres said, 'Oh, it's the same as with you, Mr Clinton – three to four million people are unhappy!'

15
MISCELLANEOUS

The world-famous Jewish painter Max Liebermann was in conversation with a very ambitious Jew. 'I've tried painting as well as poetry,' said the man. 'In your opinion, should I paint or write?'

'I would say – write,' Liebermann answered.

'Have you ever read any of my poems?'

'No, but I've seen some of your pictures!'

✡

During a conversation between Albert Einstein and Charlie Chaplin, the great physicist said to the world-famous comedian, 'What I admire most about your art is its universal quality. The whole world understands you!'

'That's right,' Chaplin replied, 'and yet your fame is much more unusual than mine: the whole world admires you and nobody understands you!'

✡

Early in this century one Jew said to another, 'Jankel, you know a lot about these things. Can you explain to me how a telegraph works? I can't understand how words can be sent along a wire.'

'Let me try to explain,' replied Jankel. 'I'll use an example. Imagine a huge dog whose head is in Brighton and whose tail is in Bristol. If someone treads on the tail in Bristol, the dog barks in Brighton. The same happens with a telegraph wire.'

'I see. Now I understand how a wire telegraph works. But how do you explain how a wireless telegraph works?'

'It's exactly the same – only without the dog!'

✡

In 1980, during the Iran-Iraq War, a rabbi was asked by a journalist what the Jews thought about this war. He answered, 'We wish both sides success!'

✡

In 1932 Jacob Horowitz was visiting his cousin in London. While on a sight-seeing tour around the city, they passed through Mayfair, and Jacob admired the magnificent houses. He said to his cousin, 'I would love to live in one of those houses!'

They arrived at Buckingham Palace, but this time the guest didn't say a word. The cousin asked him, 'And wouldn't you like to live here?'

'Of course not! Just think of the *mezuzot*¹ – they alone would cost a fortune!'

✡

An Irish Jew was visiting London. In the big synagogue he heard the Cantor ask another Jew a riddle: 'Who is my father's son and yet not my brother?'

No answer was given. Pleased with himself, the Cantor said, 'It's me, of course!'

The Irish Jew was impressed by this and decided to ask the same riddle in his synagogue in Ireland. Having returned home, he went to his synagogue, and after the service he asked the people, 'Who is my father's son and yet not my brother?'

Nobody knew the answer. Triumphantly he said, 'It's the Cantor from the big synagogue in London!'

✡

For the first time a Jewish father took his ten-year-old son to the public baths. On his father's instruction, the boy jumped into the water. It was cold, and he began to shiver. '*Oy, Papa, oy!*' he cried.

When the boy came out of the water his father took the bath towel and rubbed him until he was warm again, and happily his son said, 'Aah, Papa, aah!'

'My son, do you know the difference between a sin and cold water?' asked the father. 'I'm going to tell you. When you jumped into the cold water you first cried "*Oy!*" and then you said "*Aah!*" With a sin you first say "*Aah!*" and then you cry "*Oy!*"'

✡

In a Jewish restaurant in Paris a customer had ordered poached salmon. He tasted the fish and pulled a face.

'Waiter, this fish must have been in this restaurant for over a year!'

'Oh, I'm sorry sir, I couldn't possibly tell you, as I've only been working here for the past six months!'

✡

Two Jews were having a chat about their late friend. 'He left all his wealth to the Jewish orphanage,' said one.

'How generous – what did he leave?' asked the other.

'Eleven children!'

✡

A theatre in Vienna staged an *avant-garde* play. Old Madam Kaminski, half deaf and knowing almost no German at all, was sitting in the front row and appeared to be thoroughly enjoying the performance. The woman in the next seat asked if she could understand the play.

'Not a single word, but the spotlight is warming my aching back. It's a great pleasure!'

✡

Goldstein was telling his friend Bloomfield a Jewish joke: 'Moshe and Jacob are going to a Bar Mitzvah...'

'Always these Jewish jokes!' complained Bloomfield. 'Don't you have another type for me – Chinese, for example?'

'All right – a Chinese joke, then! One day So Long Moo and Mao Tsu Nu are going to a Bar Mitzvah...'

✡

Four explorers went to Africa to study elephants – a German, a Frenchman, an Englishman and a Jew.

After spending months in the jungle with the elephants, they returned home, and each of them wrote a book about his African experiences. The German called his book *The Feeding Habits of the Elephant and their Effect on its Life Expectancy*. The Frenchman wrote two volumes entitled *The Love Life of the Elephant*. The Englishman composed a *magnum opus* entitled *The Kingdom of the Elephant and its Gradual Incorporation into the British Commonwealth*. The Jew published a polemic essay with the title *The Elephant and the Jewish Problem*.

✡

England, in the 1900s. Foreign Minister Edward Grey was on a train to London, travelling first class. In his compartment was a Jew who was curious about the identity of his distinguished-looking travelling companion and who tried to get Grey into conversation. Yet the minister politely avoided answering all questions about his occupation.

Finally the Jew couldn't control his curiosity any further: 'I'm travelling for Feinberg and Green,' he said. 'And you – who are you travelling for?'

'For King and Country!' replied Grey.

'King and Country? Never heard of that firm – but it sounds Jewish. In which case we're colleagues! *Mazel tov*!'

✡

Two Jews from Eastern Europe were on a visit to Vienna, exploring the city with great interest. At a theatre they stopped and read the announcement for the evening's programme: 'Today we play *Hamlet or the Prince of Denmark*!'

Moshe shrugged his shoulders. 'Strange people, these Vienna actors,' he said. 'It's the afternoon, and they still haven't decided what they're going to play in the evening!'

✡

A Jewish woman had filed a petition for divorce. In court her Jewish solicitor explained the case to the judge:

'Your Honour, there is no way this woman can put up with her husband's behaviour. He drinks like Lot, is sinful like Haman and curses like Balaam!'

'The divorce is hereby granted,' declared the judge. He turned to the woman: 'And let's hope that your husband's dangerous colleagues, mentioned by your solicitor, get caught and brought to justice too!'

✡

A Jewish girl who was studying the history of art at London University planned a trip to Italy to see some famous works of art for real. Since nobody was willing to look after her grandmother, with whom she shared a flat, the girl took her granny with her to Italy.

In the Sistine Chapel she pointed towards the ceiling and said, 'Grandma, Michelangelo took four entire years to get this ceiling painted!'

'*Oy, vay!* He must have the same landlord that we've got!'

✡

In a grammar lesson in a German primary school the teacher asked, 'How many articles are there?'

Davidele replied, 'Two, Sir!'

'Why only two? Who says so?'

'My father, Sir. He's a grocer and he always says, "There are only two articles – those that sell and those that don't!"'

✡

'How is our little Goldie doing at school?' the girl's father asked his wife.

'I didn't want to tell you,' replied the mother, 'but her Geography teacher punished her yesterday for forgetting where the Dardanelles are.'

'This girl – *oy!* Last week she couldn't remember where Gibraltar is and this week she's forgotten where the Dardanelles are – even though I've told her a hundred times, "Goldie, do pay attention to where you put your things!"'

✡

A Jewish couple booked a holiday flat at the Riviera for a whole month. During the first week they were visited by a young Jew from Paris, a slight acquaintance of the couple. Expecting him to leave again soon, they welcomed him with open arms. However, the young man didn't think of leaving – he stayed one week, two weeks, and the couple were getting desperate for a polite way of showing him the door. Finally they decided to stage a marital row, hoping that their unwanted guest would get involved and take sides with one or the other of them. This would then be a good enough reason for the other half to tell him to go.

The following day the couple started the row over lunch. They shouted and hurled abuse at each other. The guest remained unmoved and ate peacefully as if nothing was happening. The husband cried, 'How can you stay so calm when you hear my wife abusing me so viciously?!'

The guest answered, 'Since I intend to stay another couple of weeks with you, I'd better not get involved in your row!'

---

[1] *Mezuzot* (small boxes containing verses from the book of Deuteronomy) are fixed to the right-hand side of doors in Jewish homes.